EINKAUFSWAGEN
SHOPPING CARTS

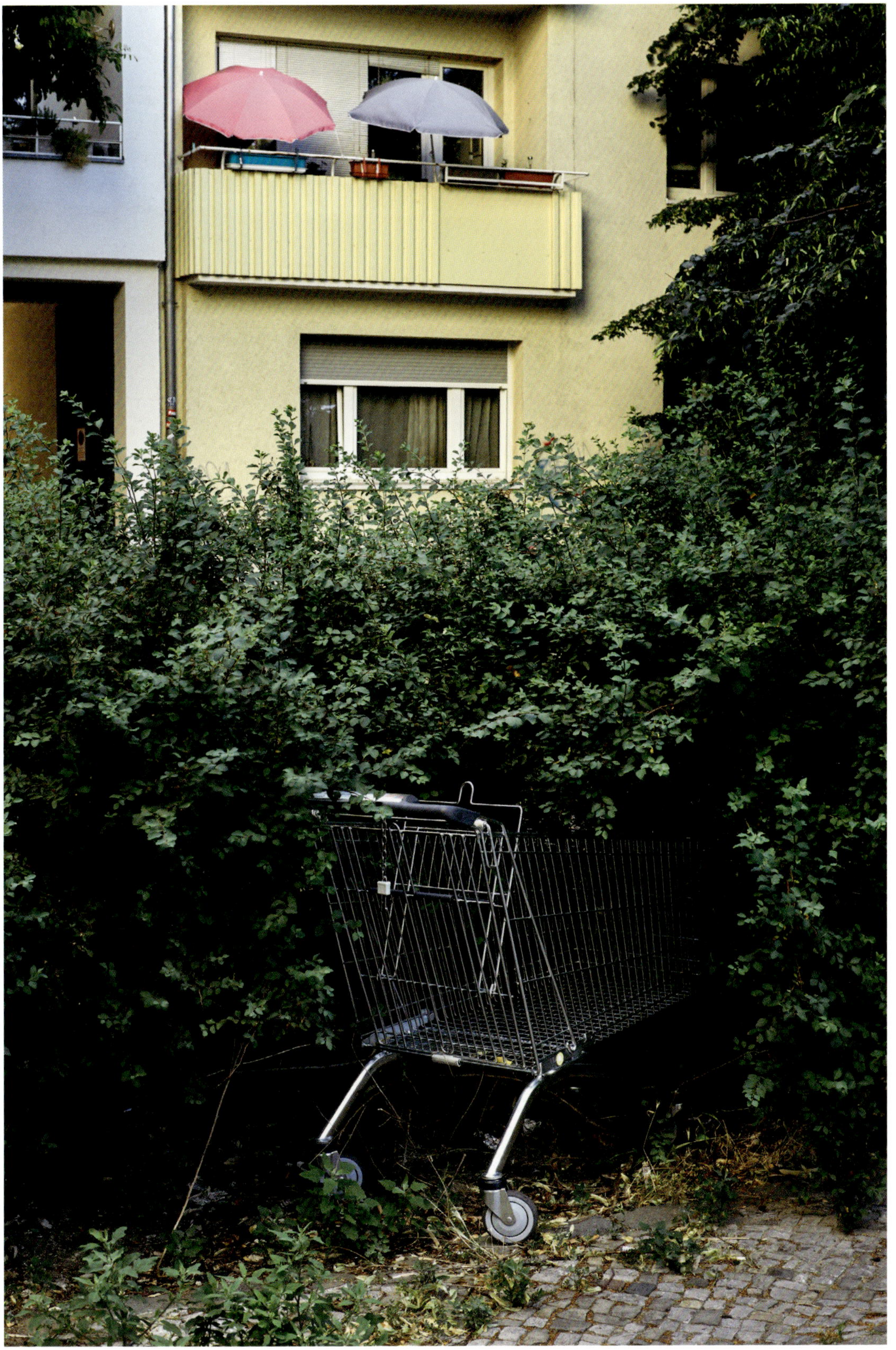

EINKAUFSWAGEN
SHOPPING CARTS

Luca Ellena

KERBER PHOTO

Einführung

Tina Wessel

Einkaufswagen: Streng formatiert stehen sie in Reih und Glied vor dem Supermarkt, allzeit einsatzbereit, um uns beim Warentransport zu Diensten zu sein. Doch manchmal werden diese praktischen Konsumhelfer der vertrauten Ordnung entrissen und gehen an den ungewöhnlichsten Orten neue Symbiosen ein – umgestoßen und auf den Kopf gestellt, an Zäunen hängend und an Büsche geschmiegt, mit kuriosen Dingen beladen und zweckentfremdet. Nicht selten begegnet man ihnen gleich paarweise, wie im Dialog vertieft und regelrecht verschmolzen mit ihrer neuen Umgebung.

Über drei Jahre hat der Fotograf Luca Ellena die deplatzierten Einkaufswagen im Berliner Stadtbild aufgespürt und diese skulpturalen Objekte in ihren oft skurrilen Posen für uns festgehalten.

Introduction

Tina Wessel

Shopping carts: they stand neatly in a row in front of supermarkets, always prepared to be of service to transport goods for us. Yet sometimes these practical aids to our consumption are yanked from their trusty environment and take on a new symbiotic relationship to unusual places: knocked over, upside down, hung on fences and propped against bushes, filled with curious things and alienated. It is not at all rare to encounter them as a duo-pack, deep in a couple-like dialogue and often blended into their surroundings.

For over three years the photographer Luca Ellena has been on the trail of such displaced shopping carts and their impact on Berlin's cityscape, and has recorded these sculptural objects in all their bizarre poses.

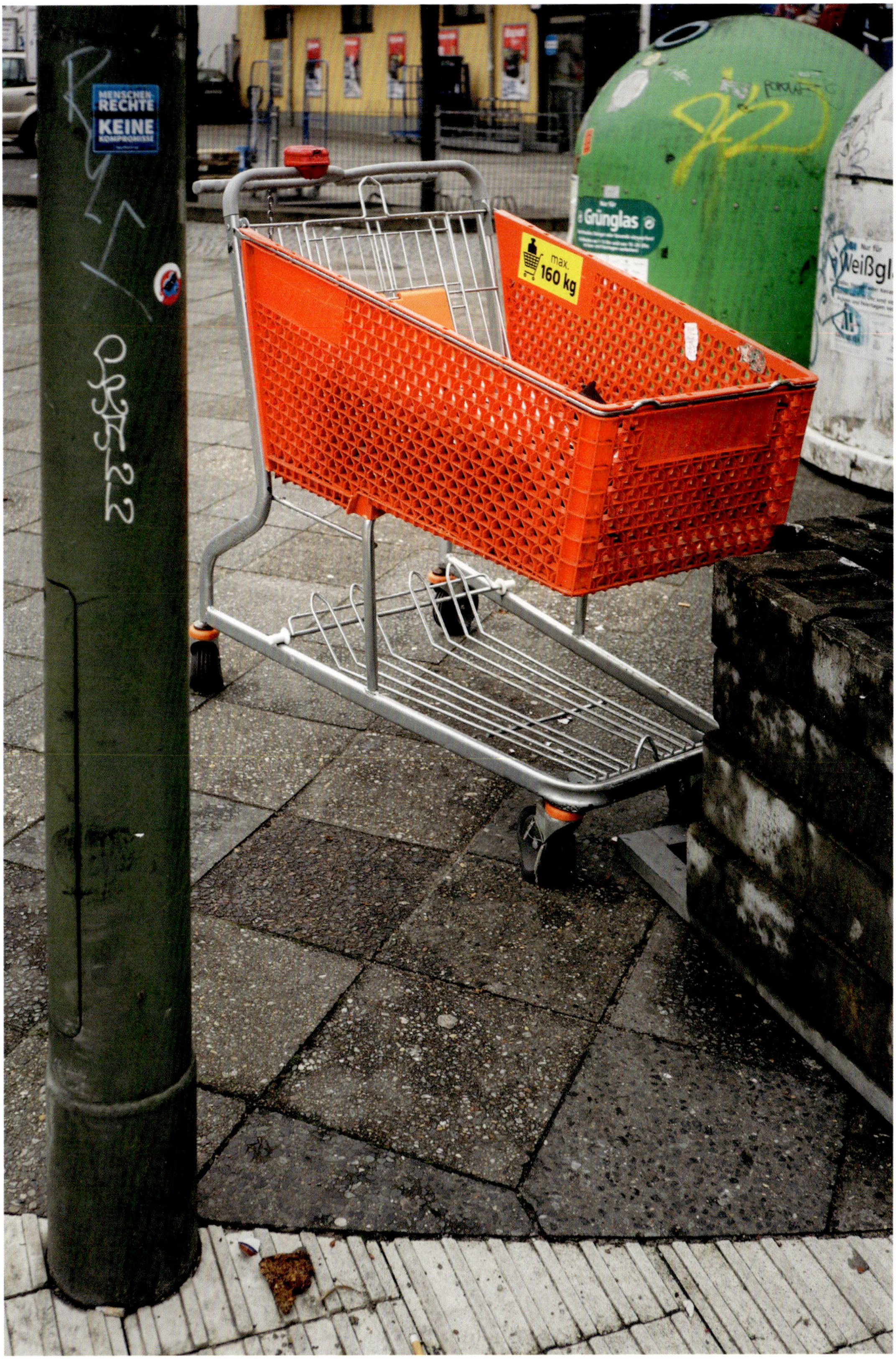
MENSCHEN-RECHTE
KEINE
KOMPROMISSE
max.
160 kg
Grünglas

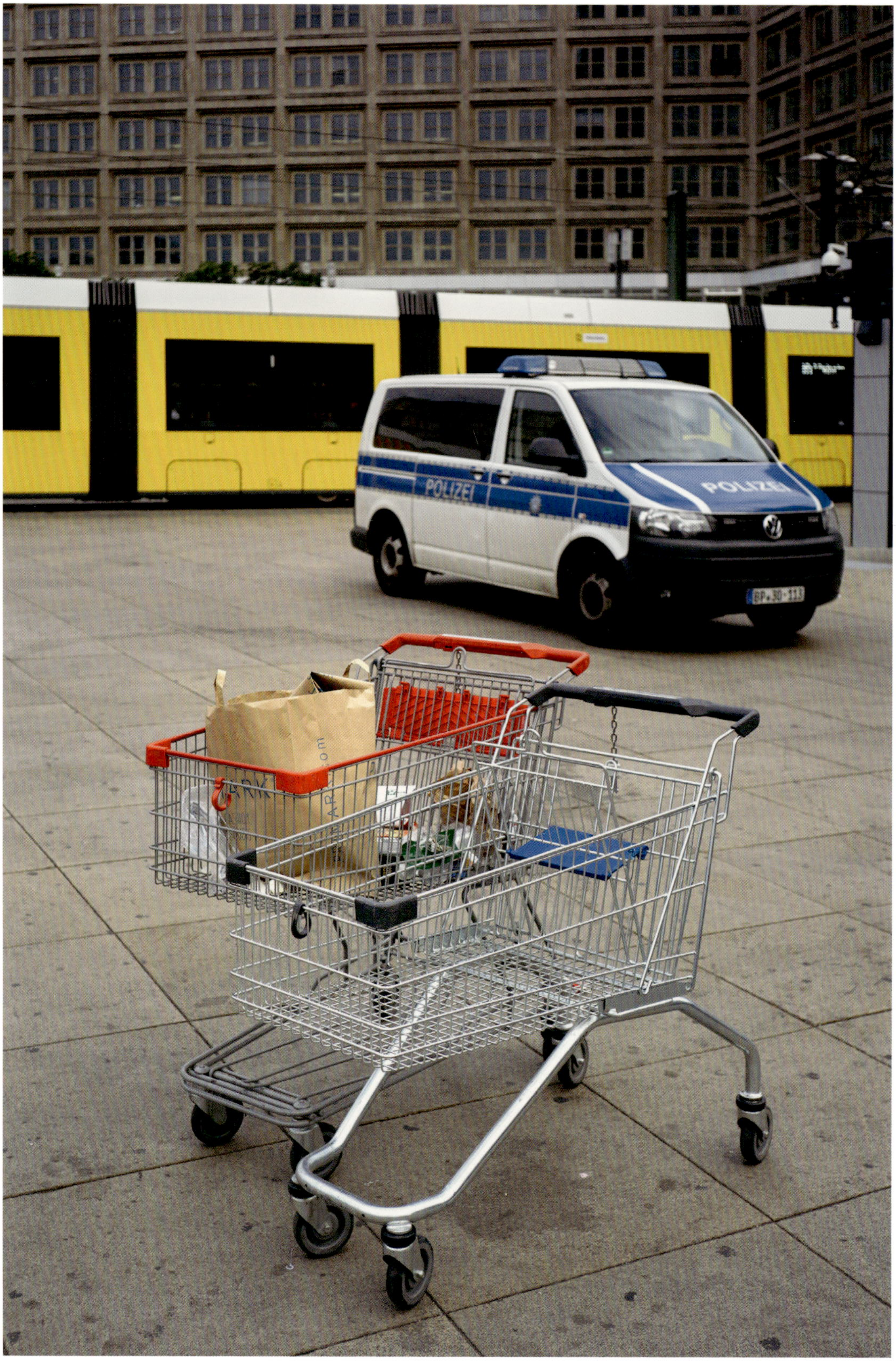
POLIZEI
POLIZEI

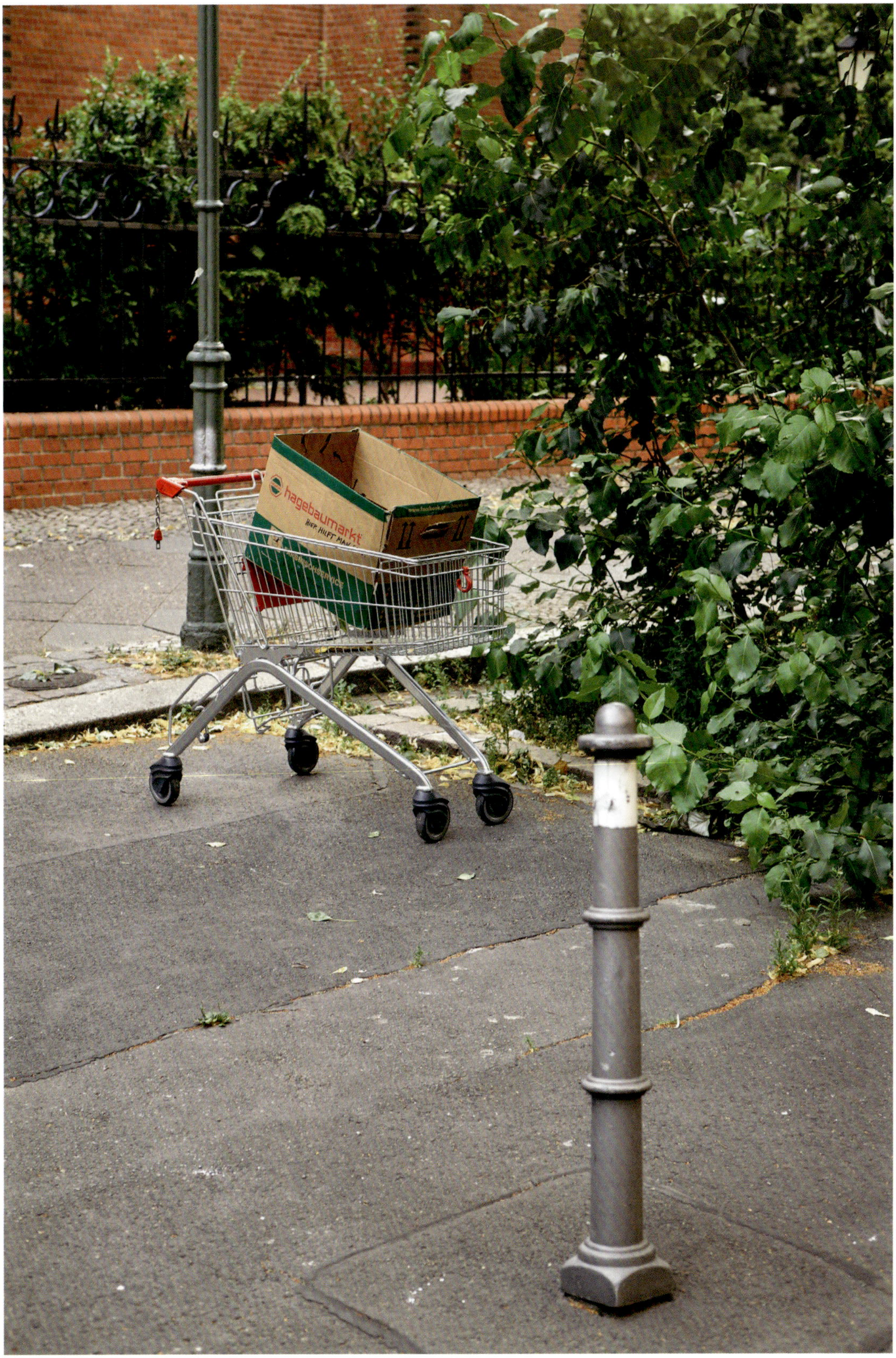
hagebaumarkt

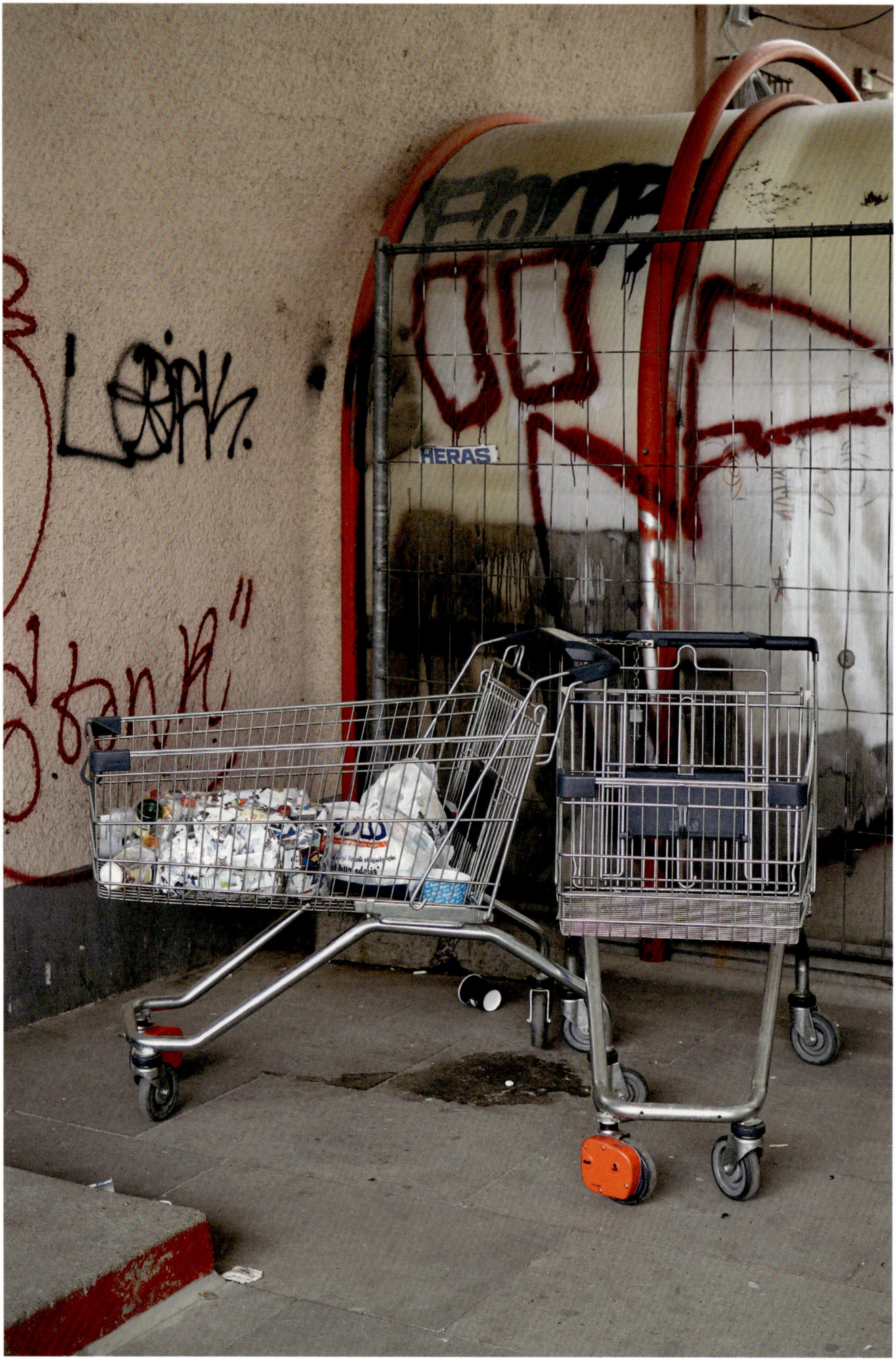
HERAS

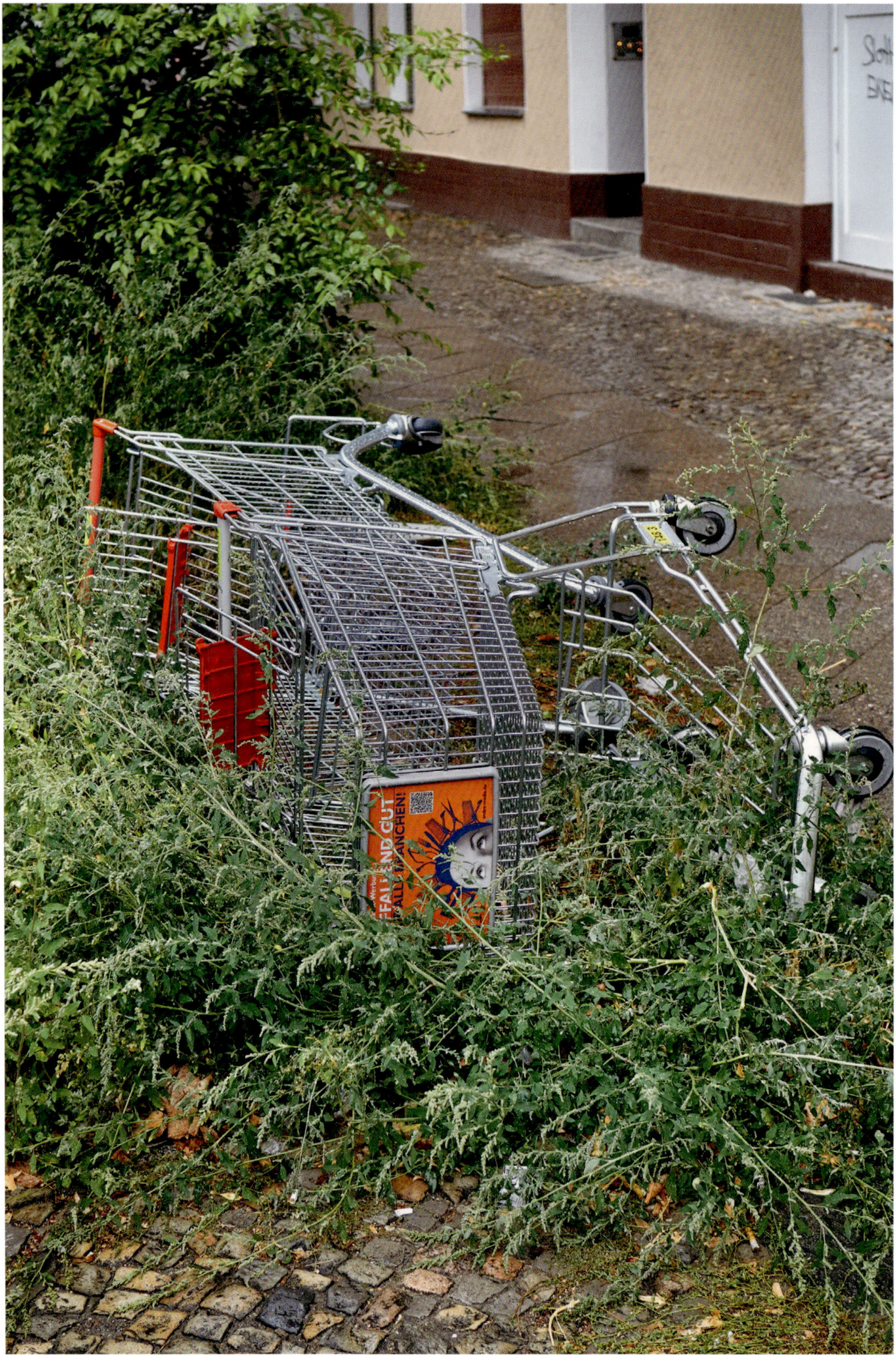

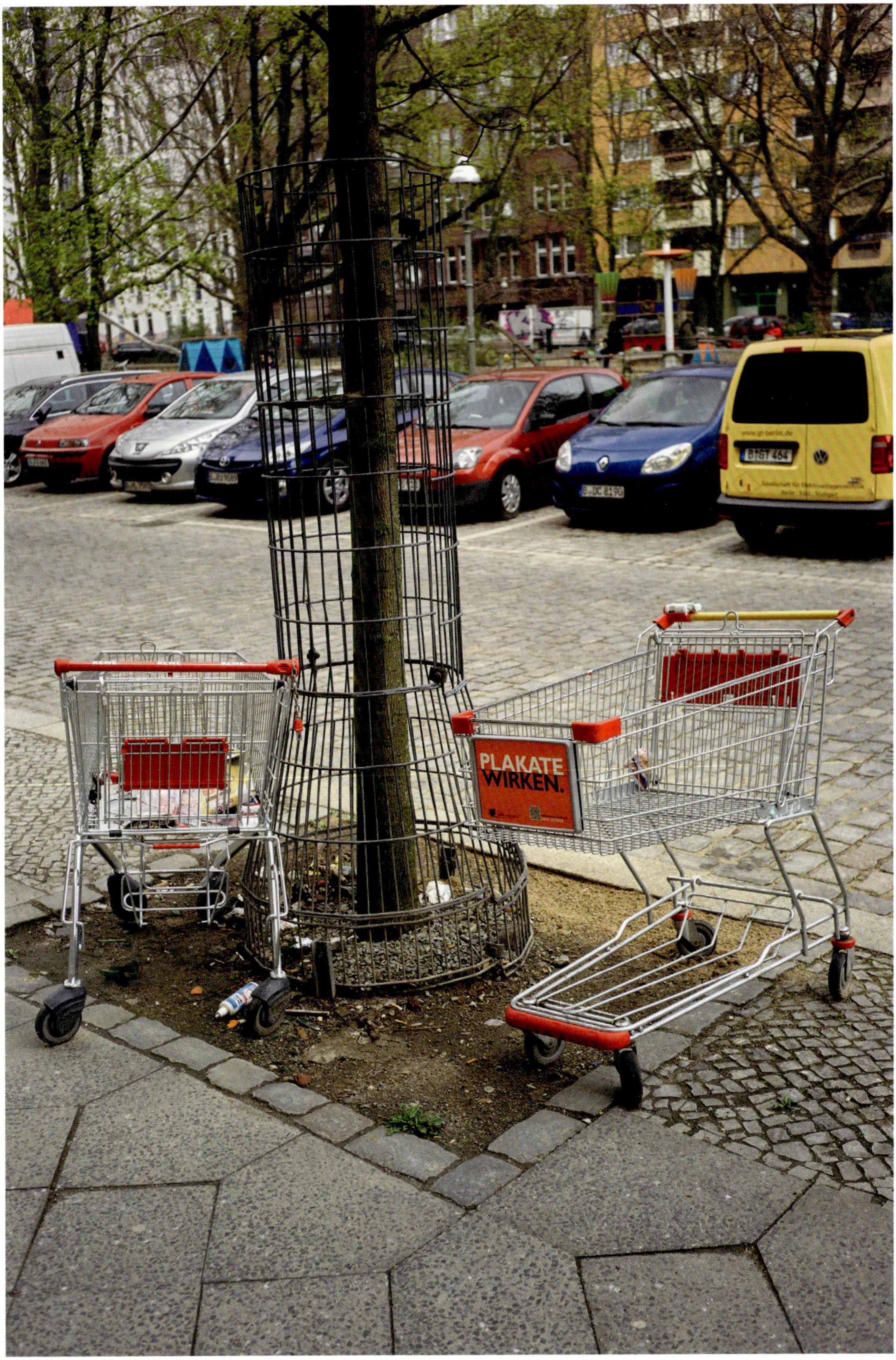
PLAKATE
WIRKEN.

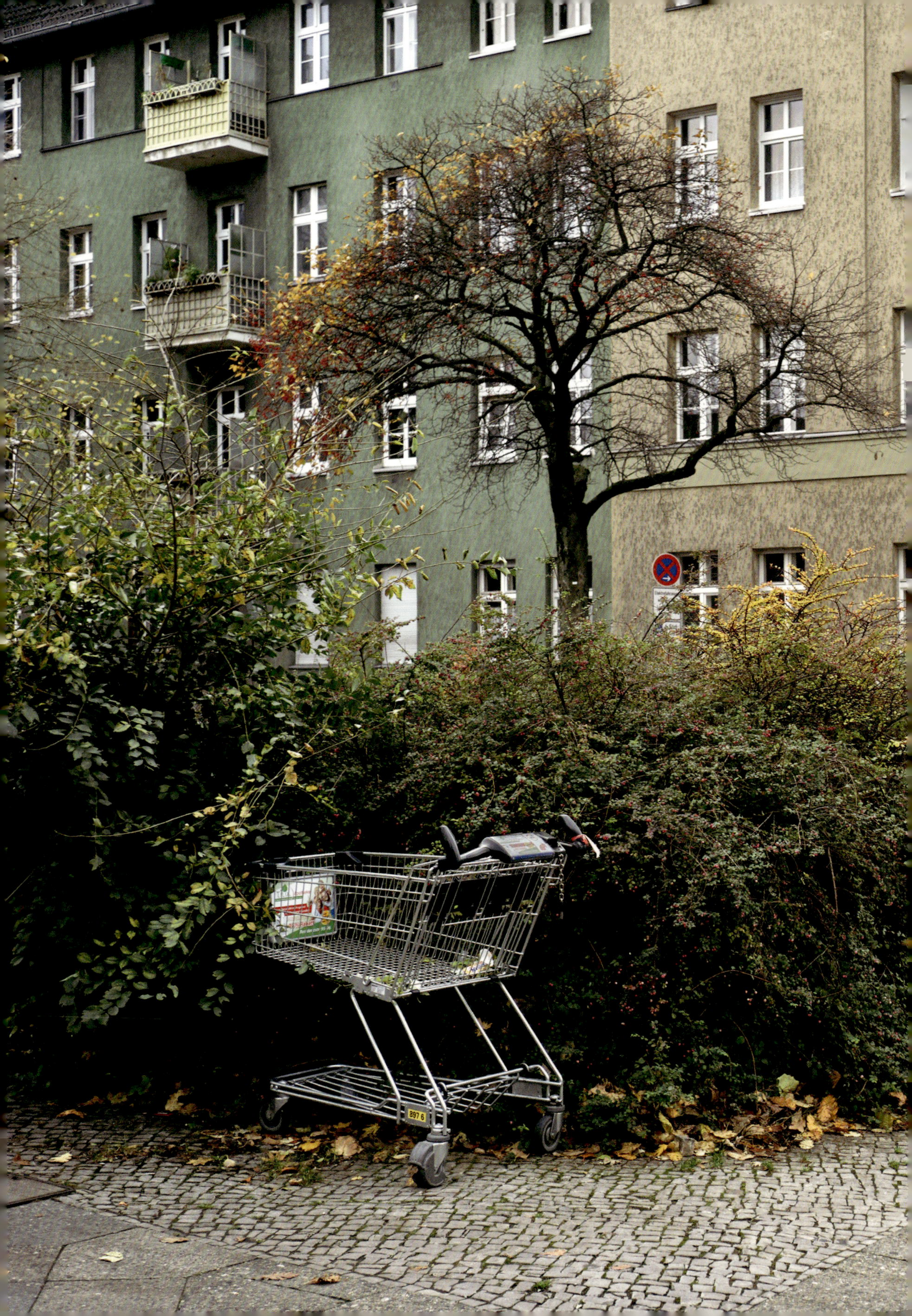

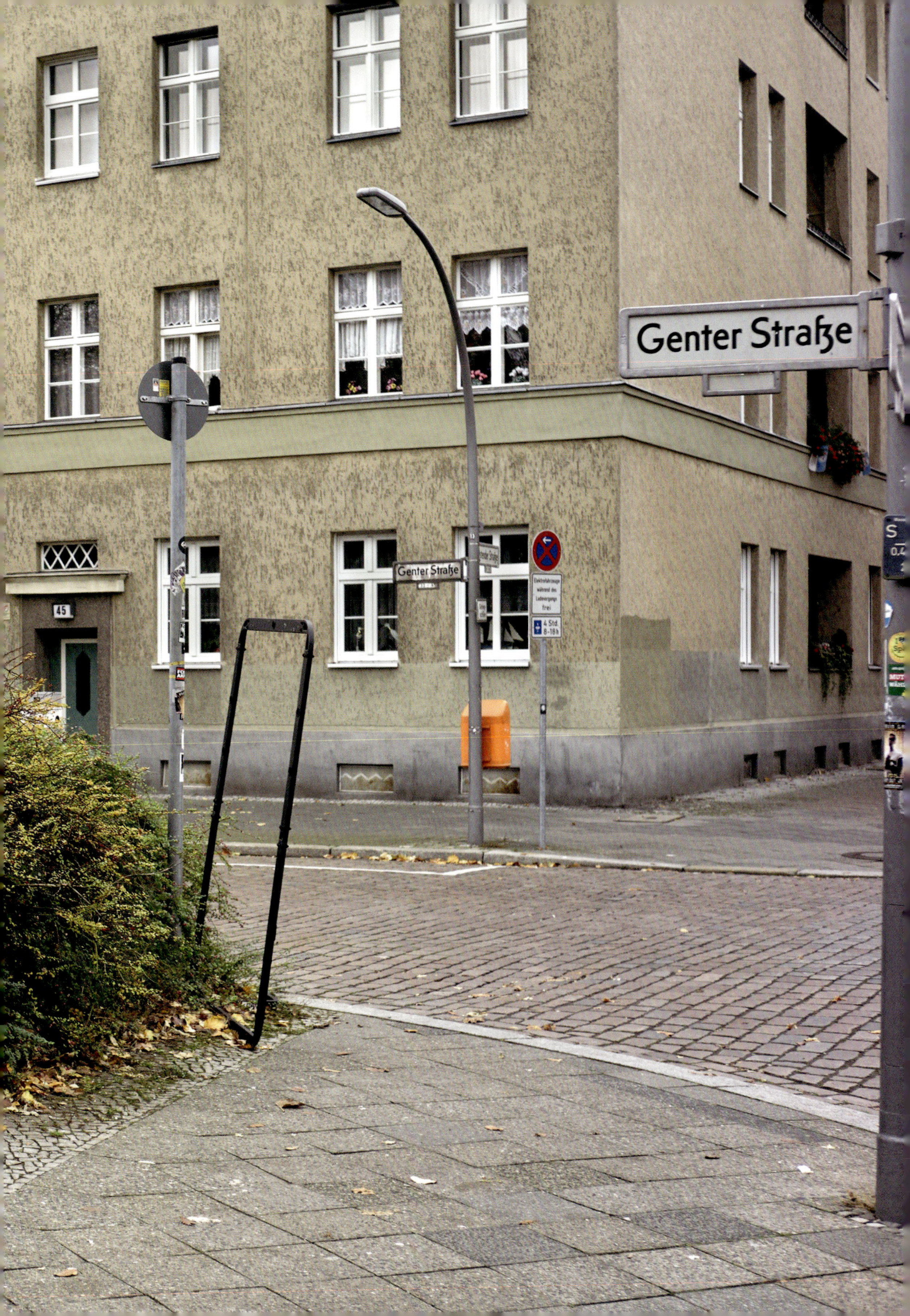
Genter Straße

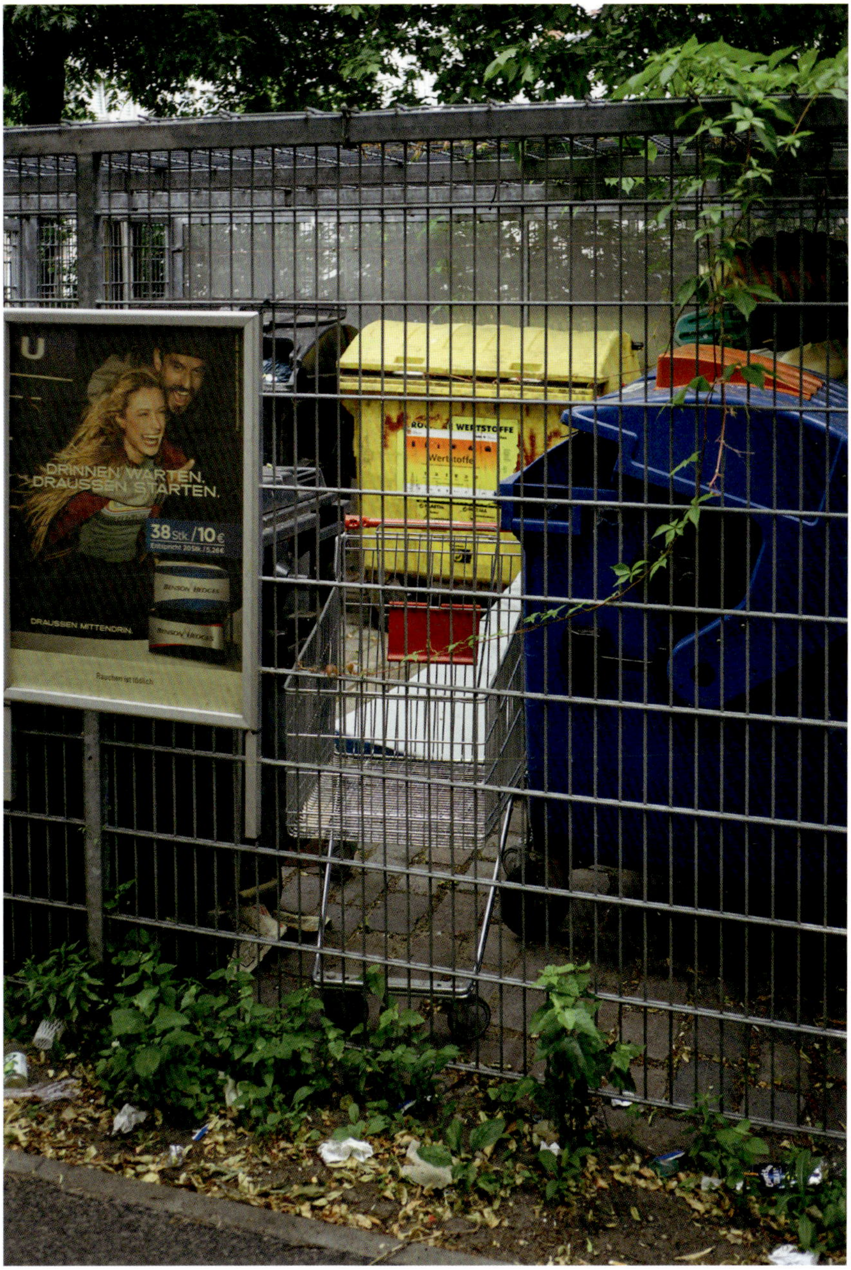
DRINNEN WARTEN.
DRAUSSEN STARTEN.
38 Stk. / 10 €
DRAUSSEN MITTENDRIN.
Rauchen ist tödlich
WERTSTOFFE
Wertstoffe

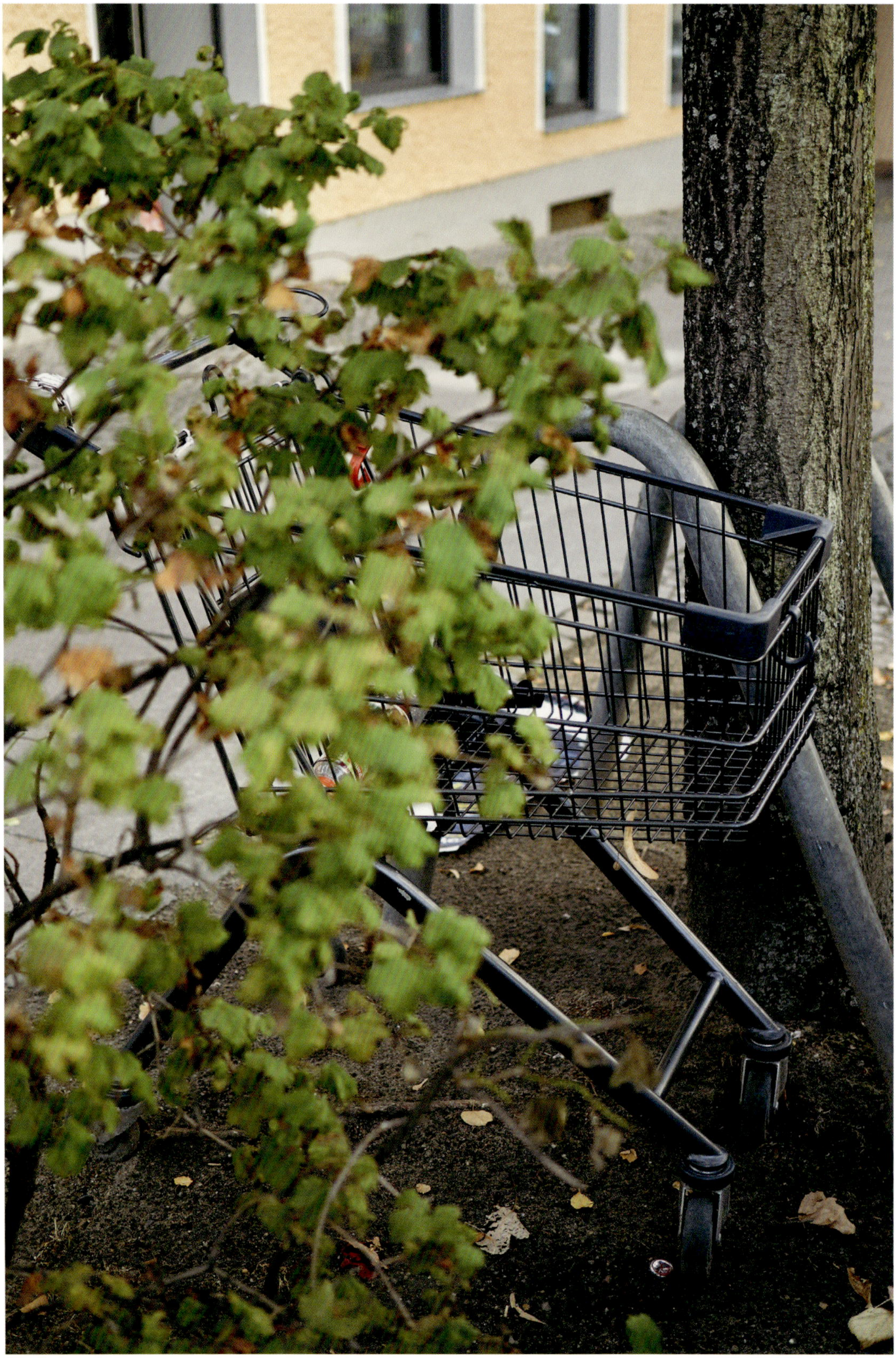

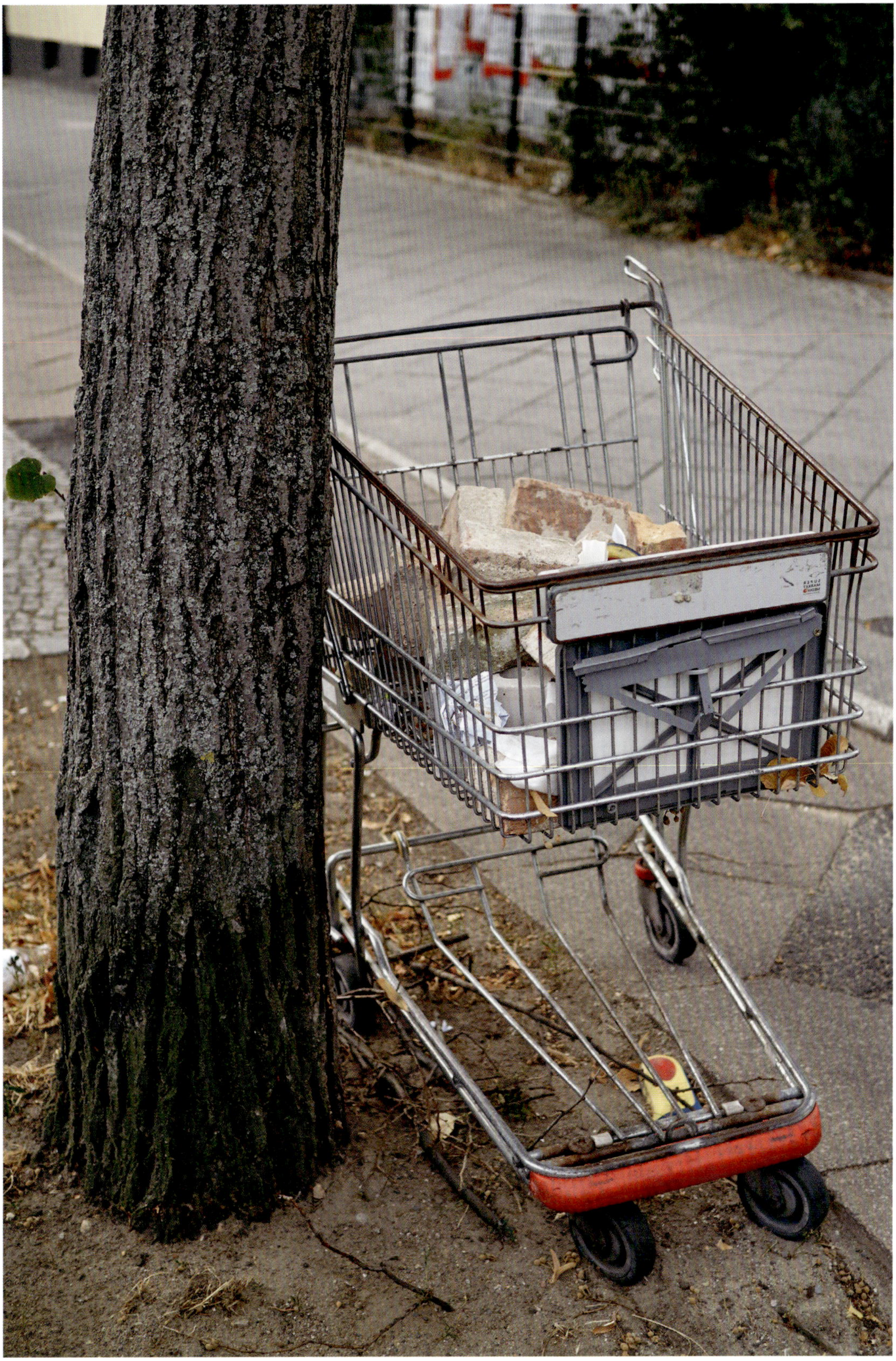

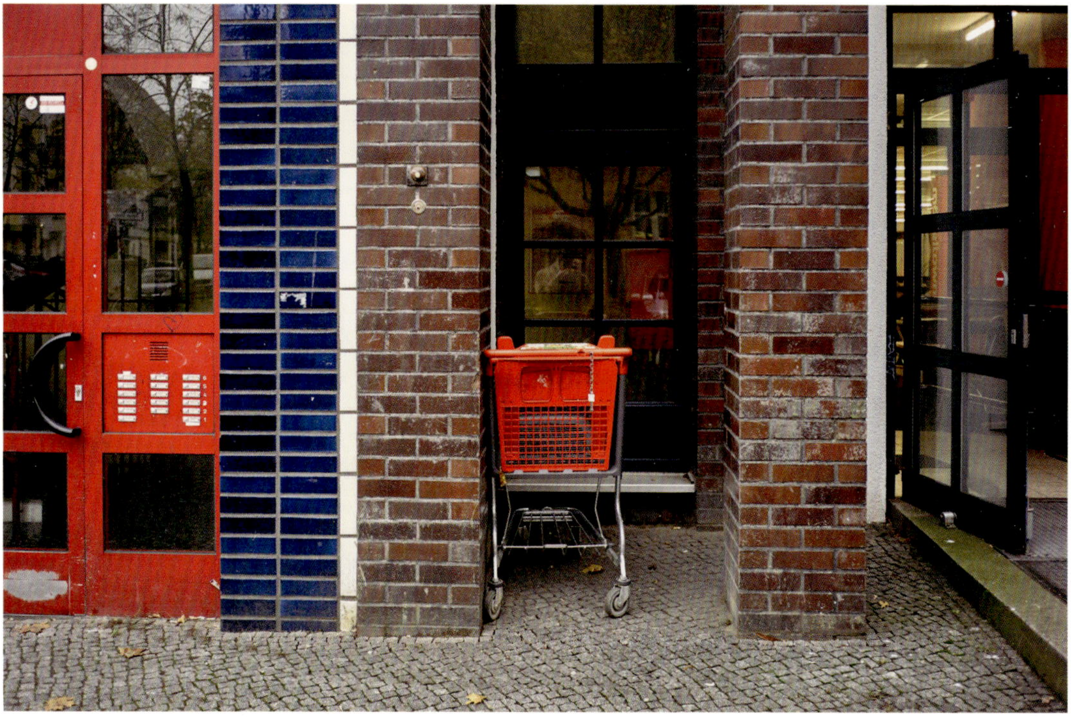

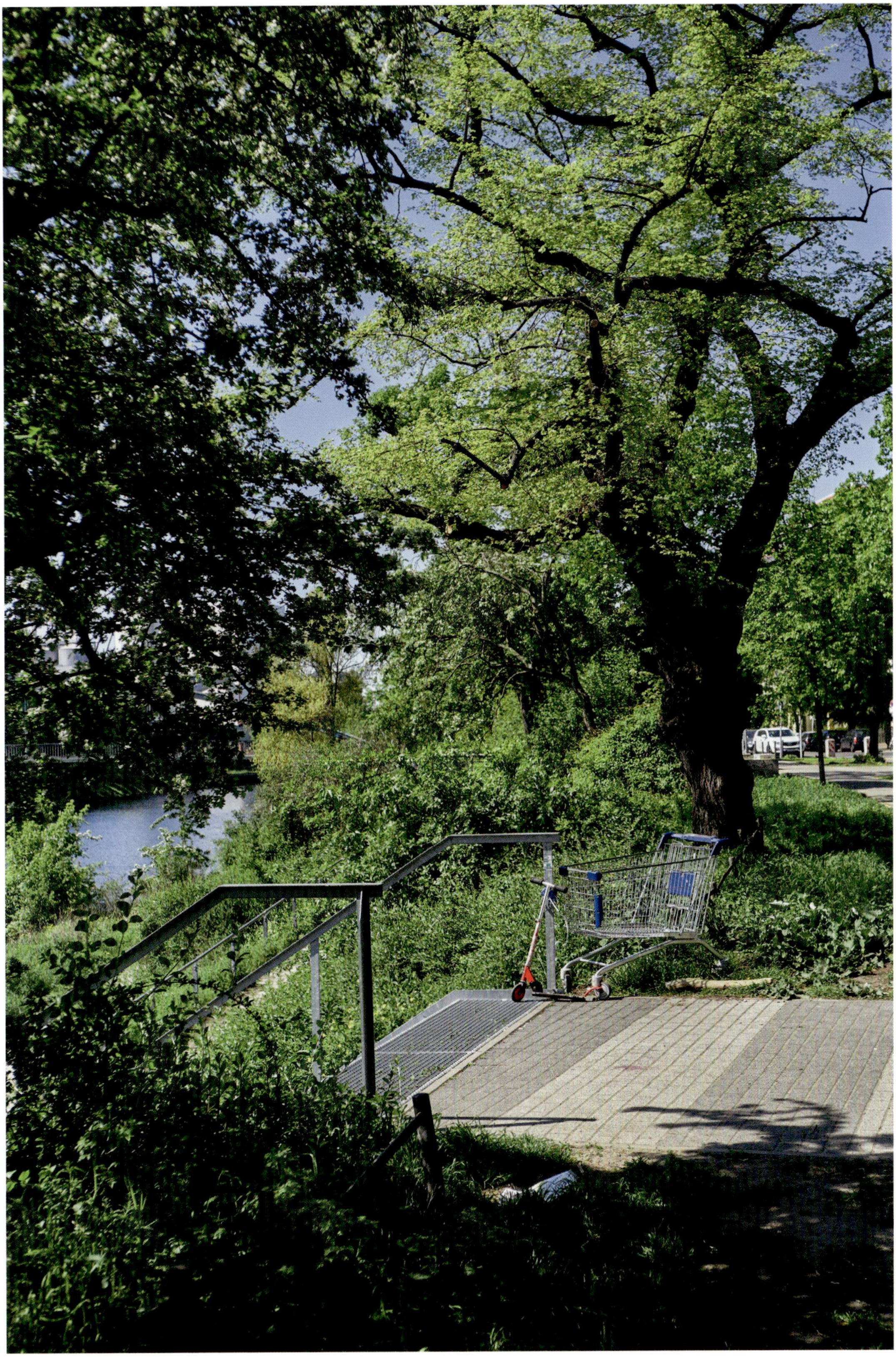

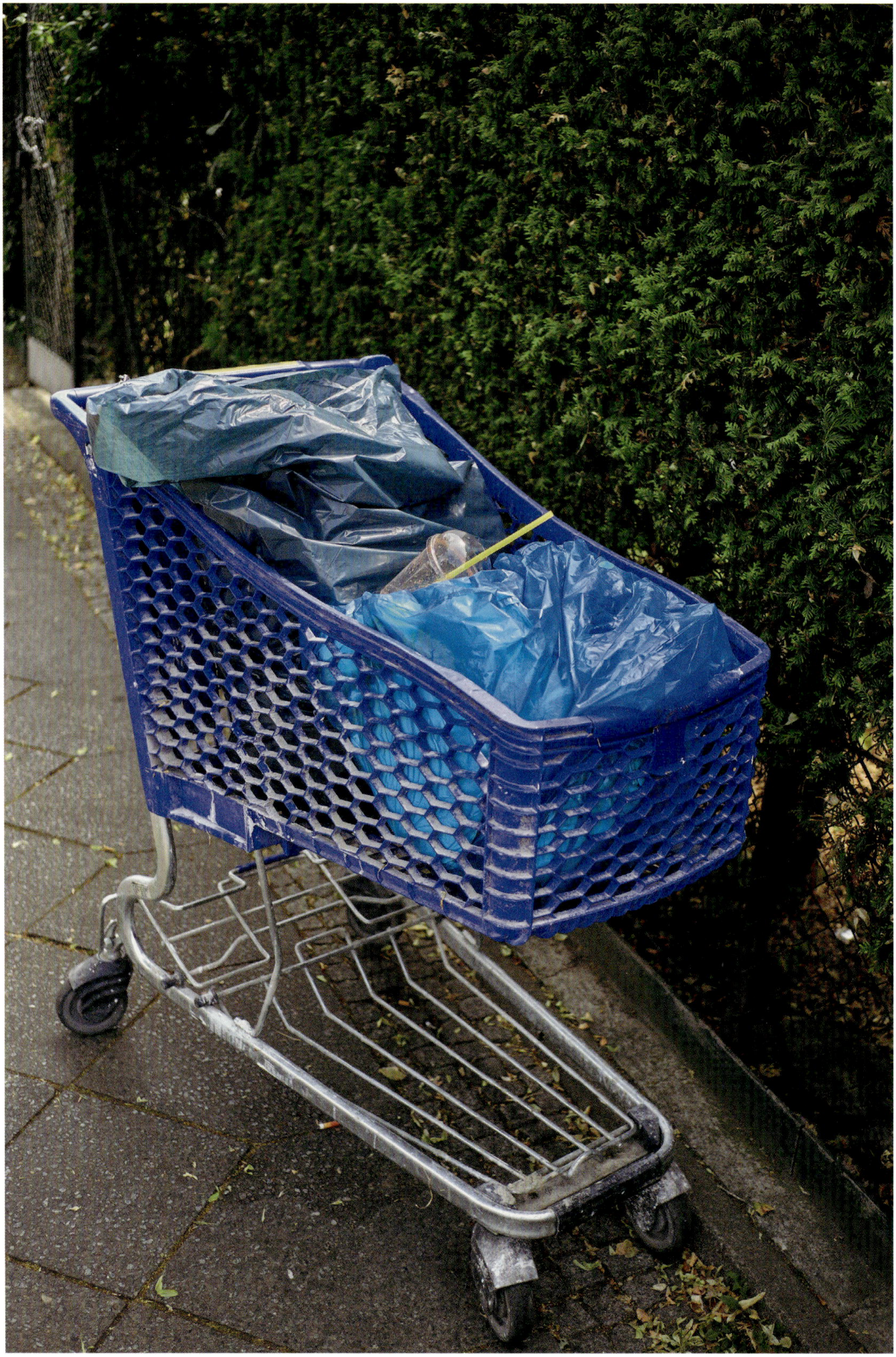

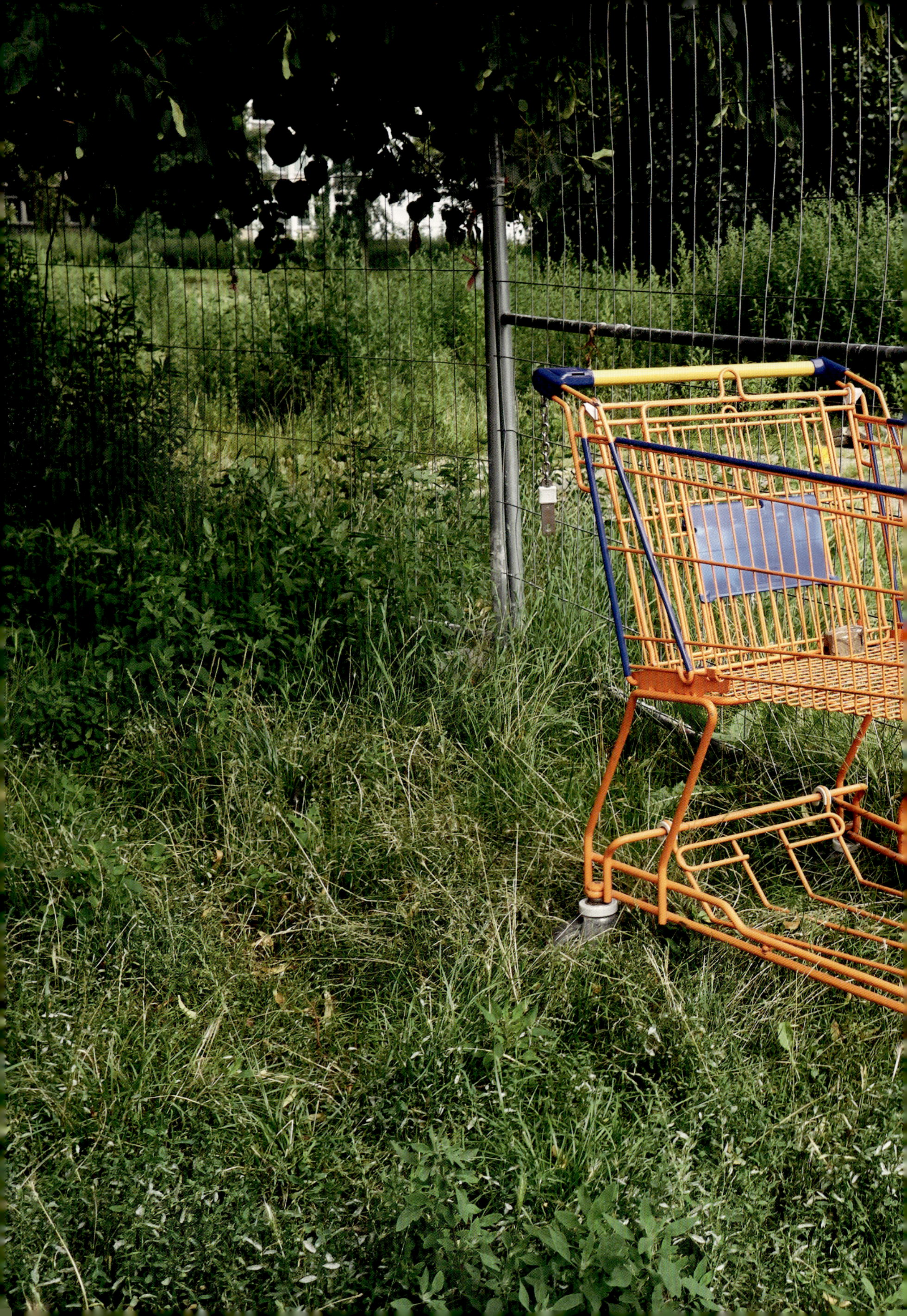

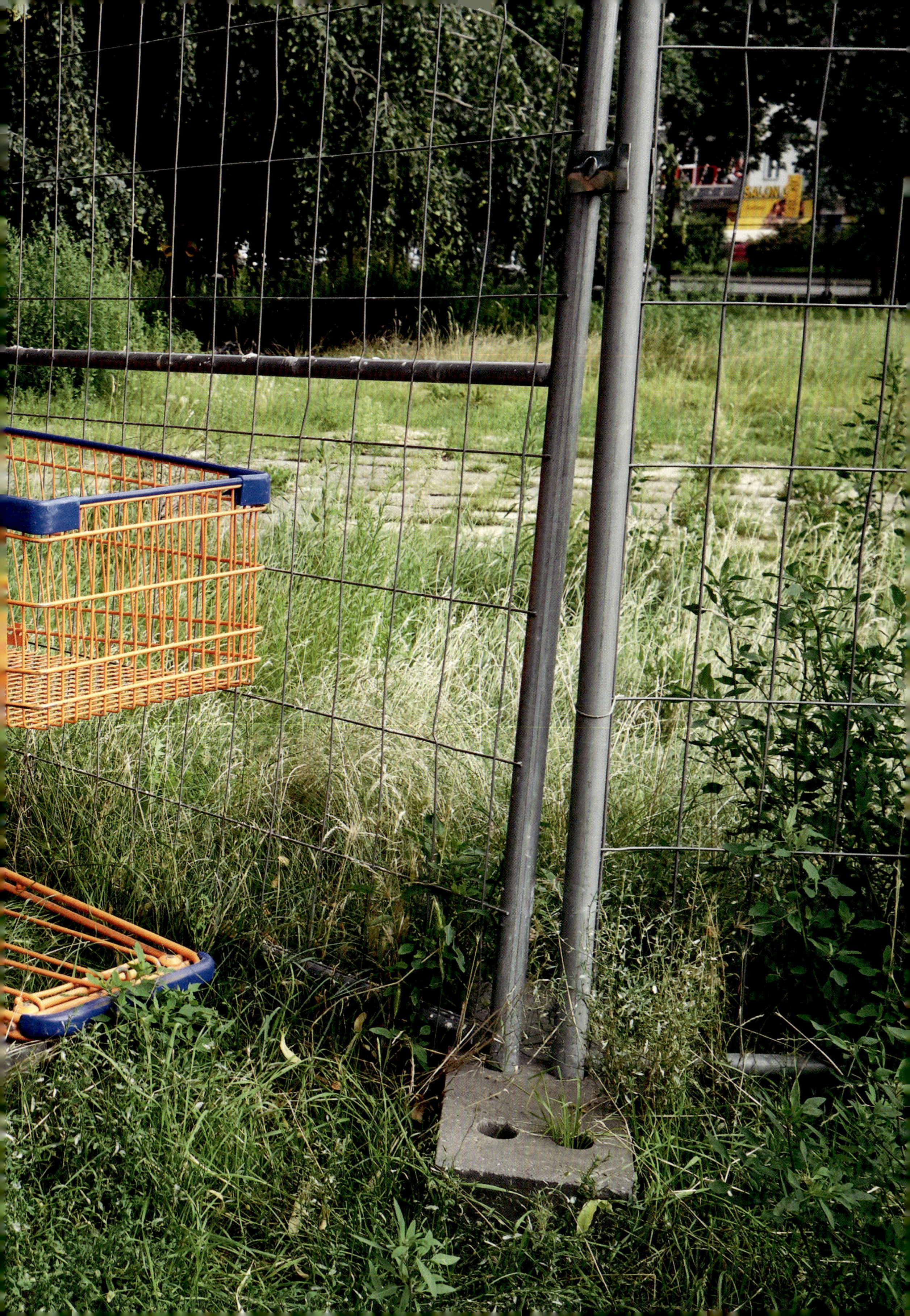
SALON

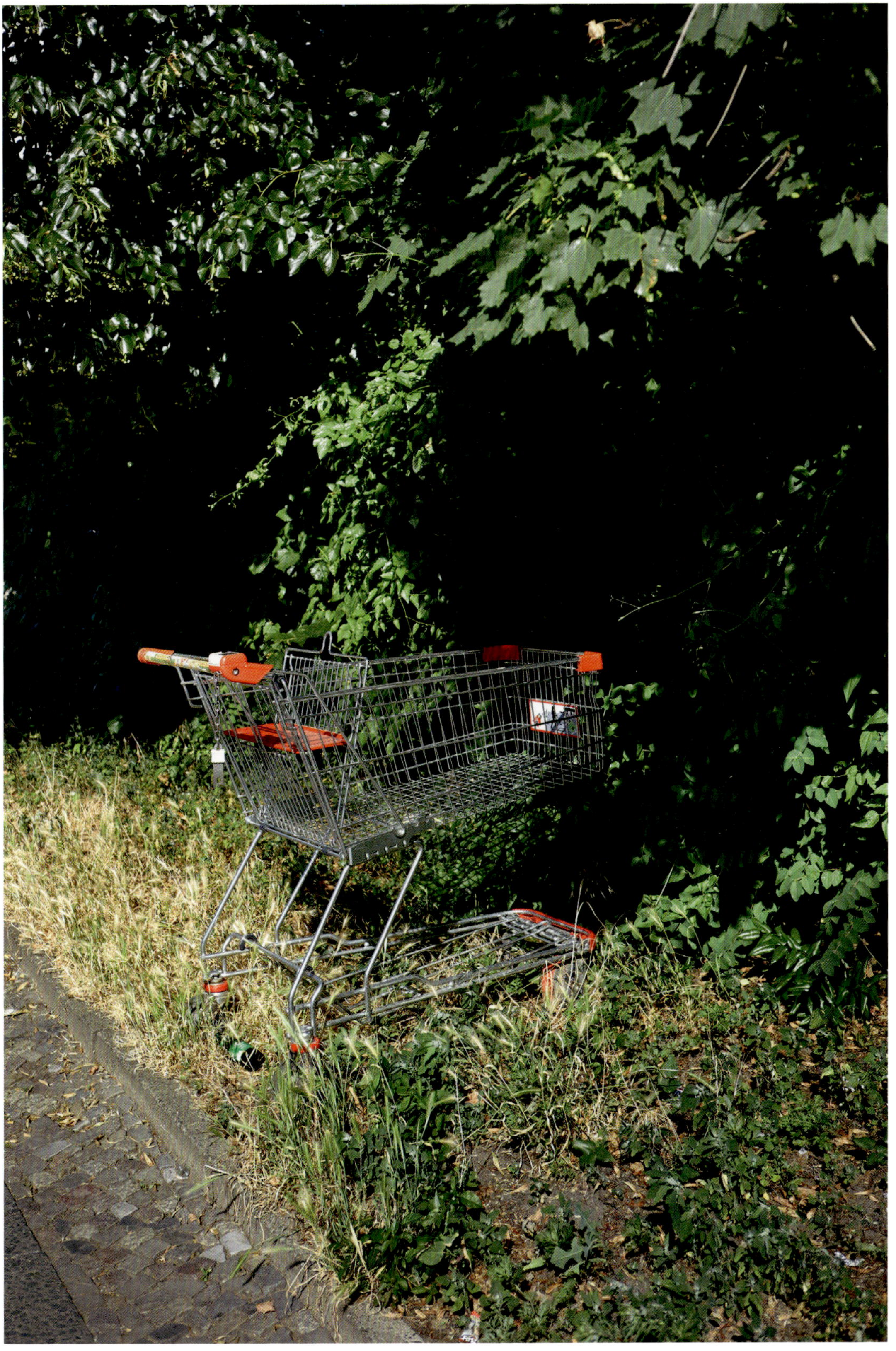

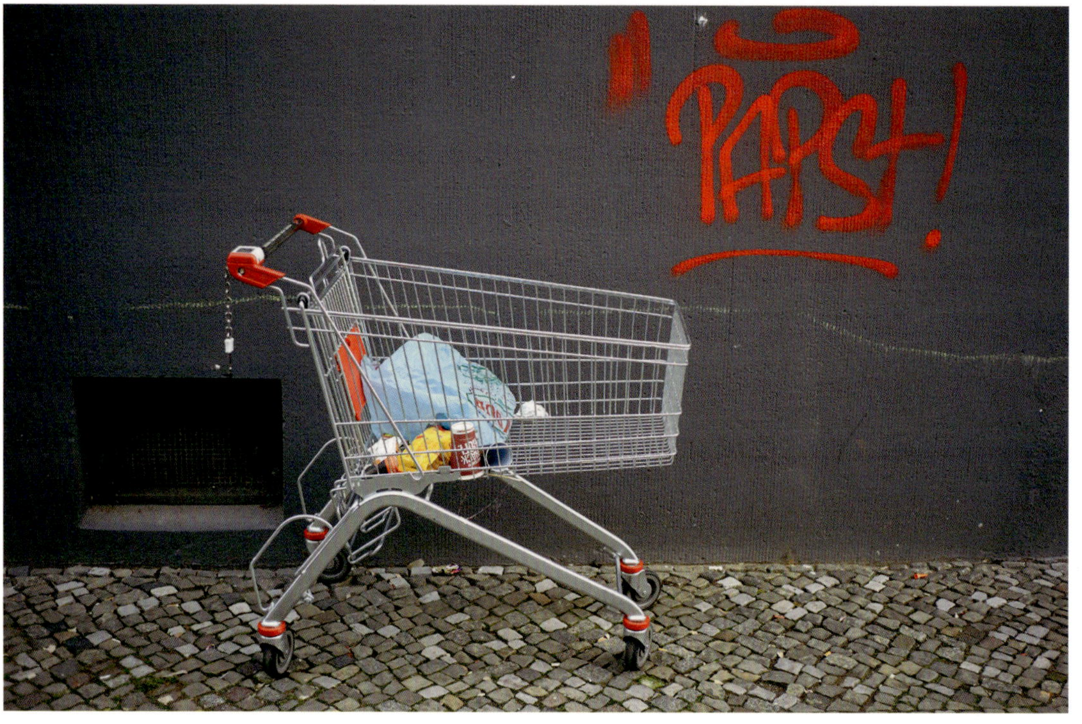
PAPST!

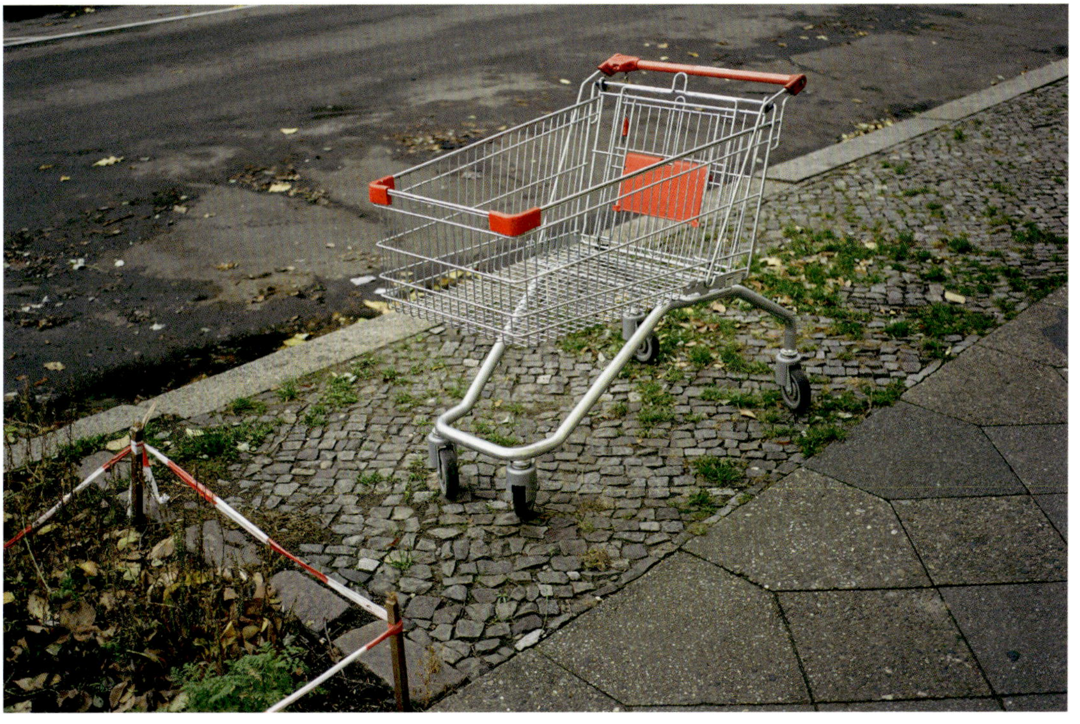

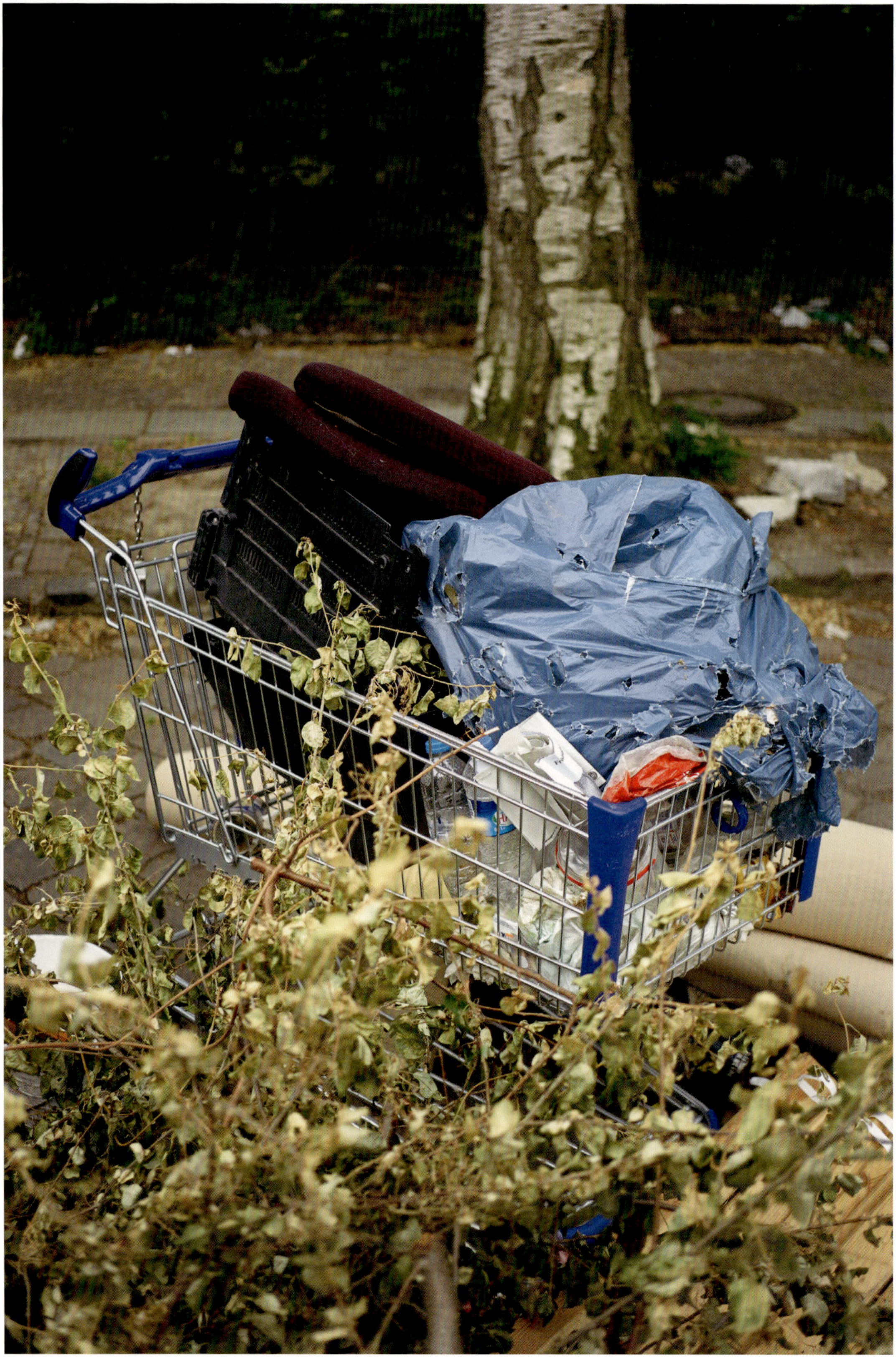

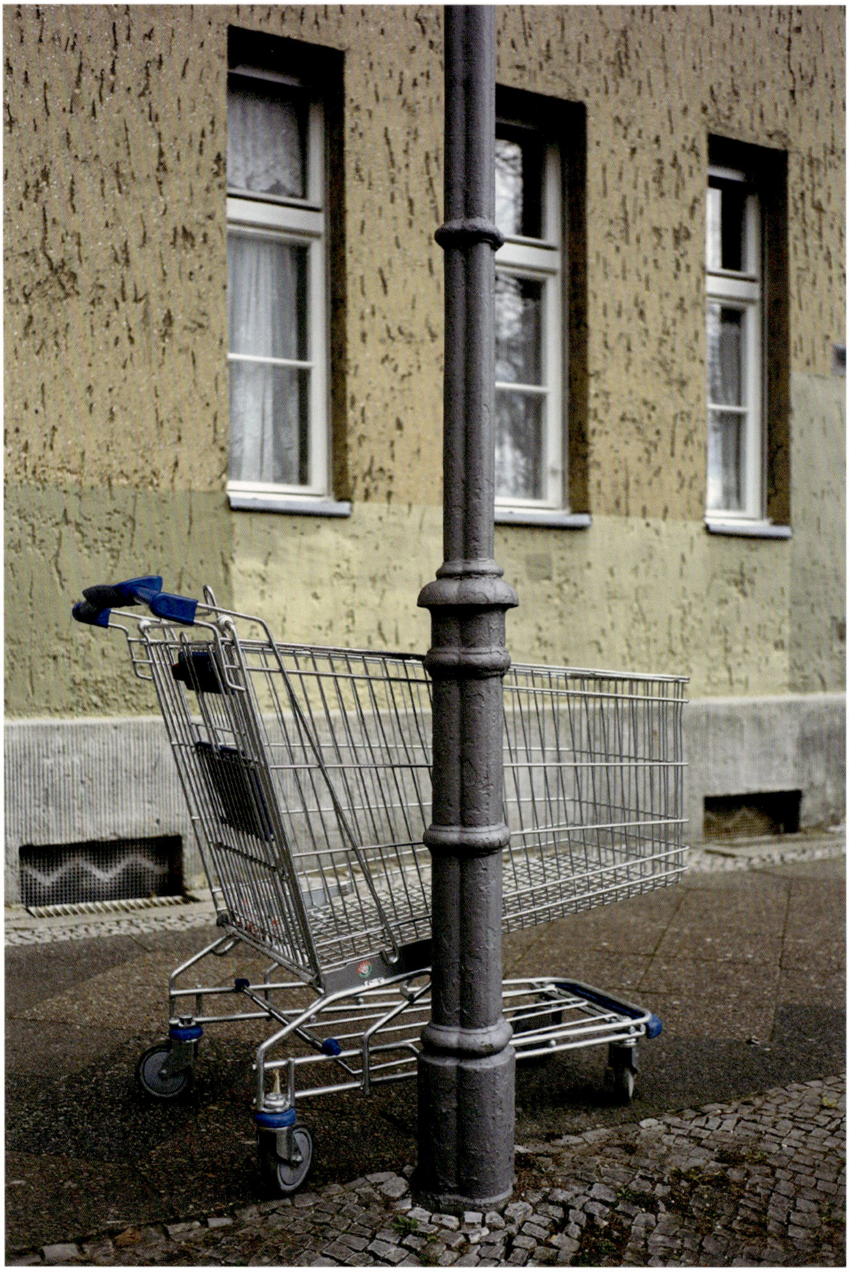

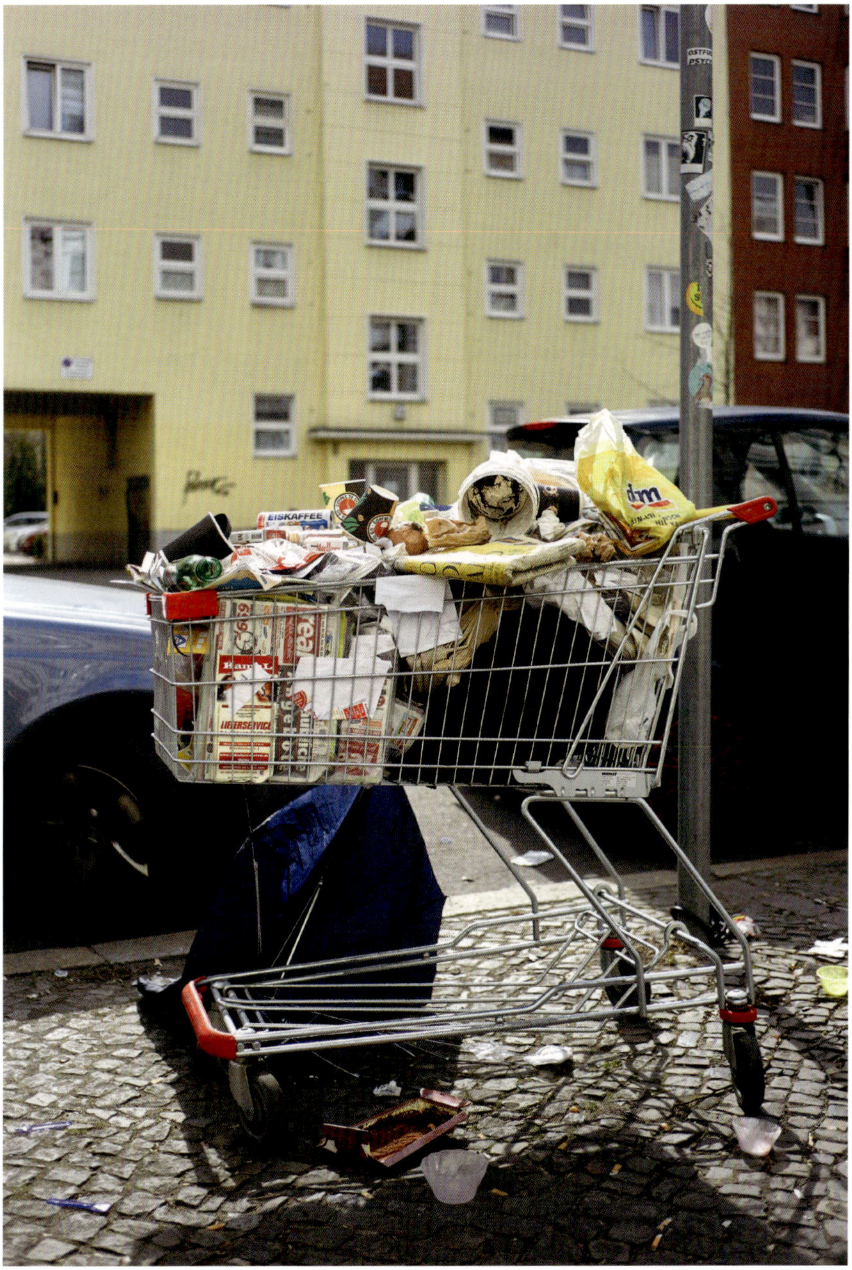
EISKAFFEE
dm

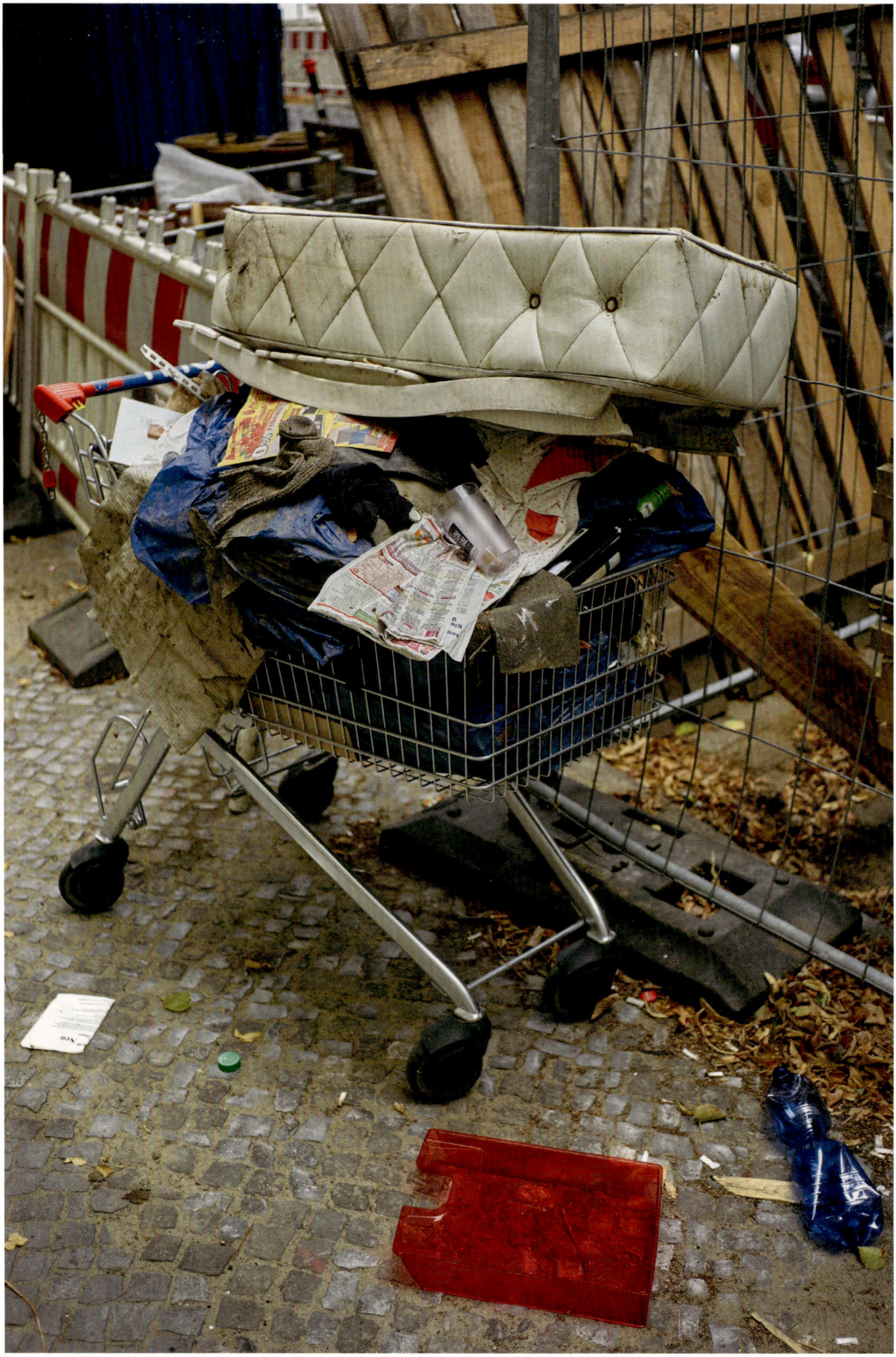

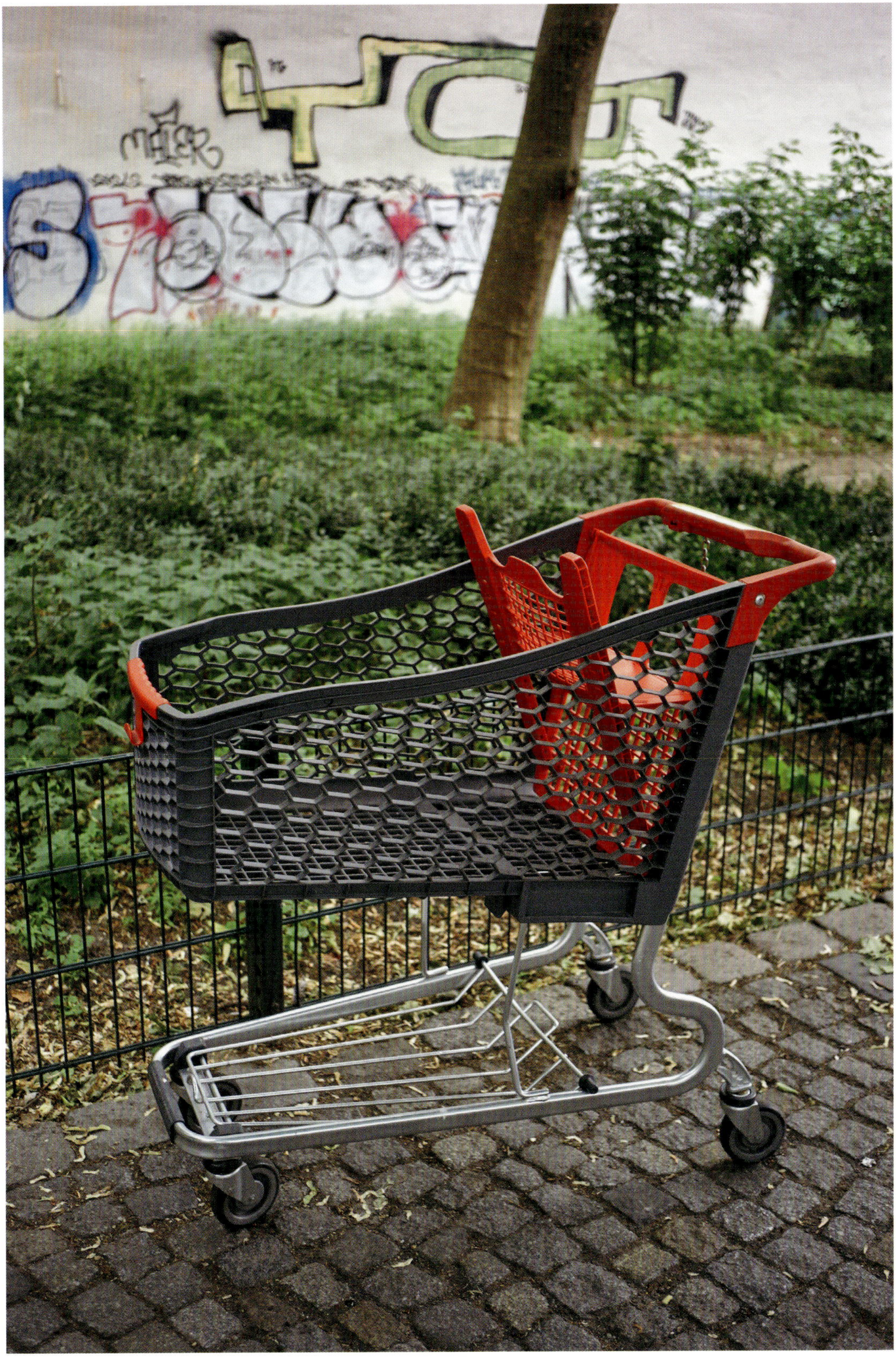

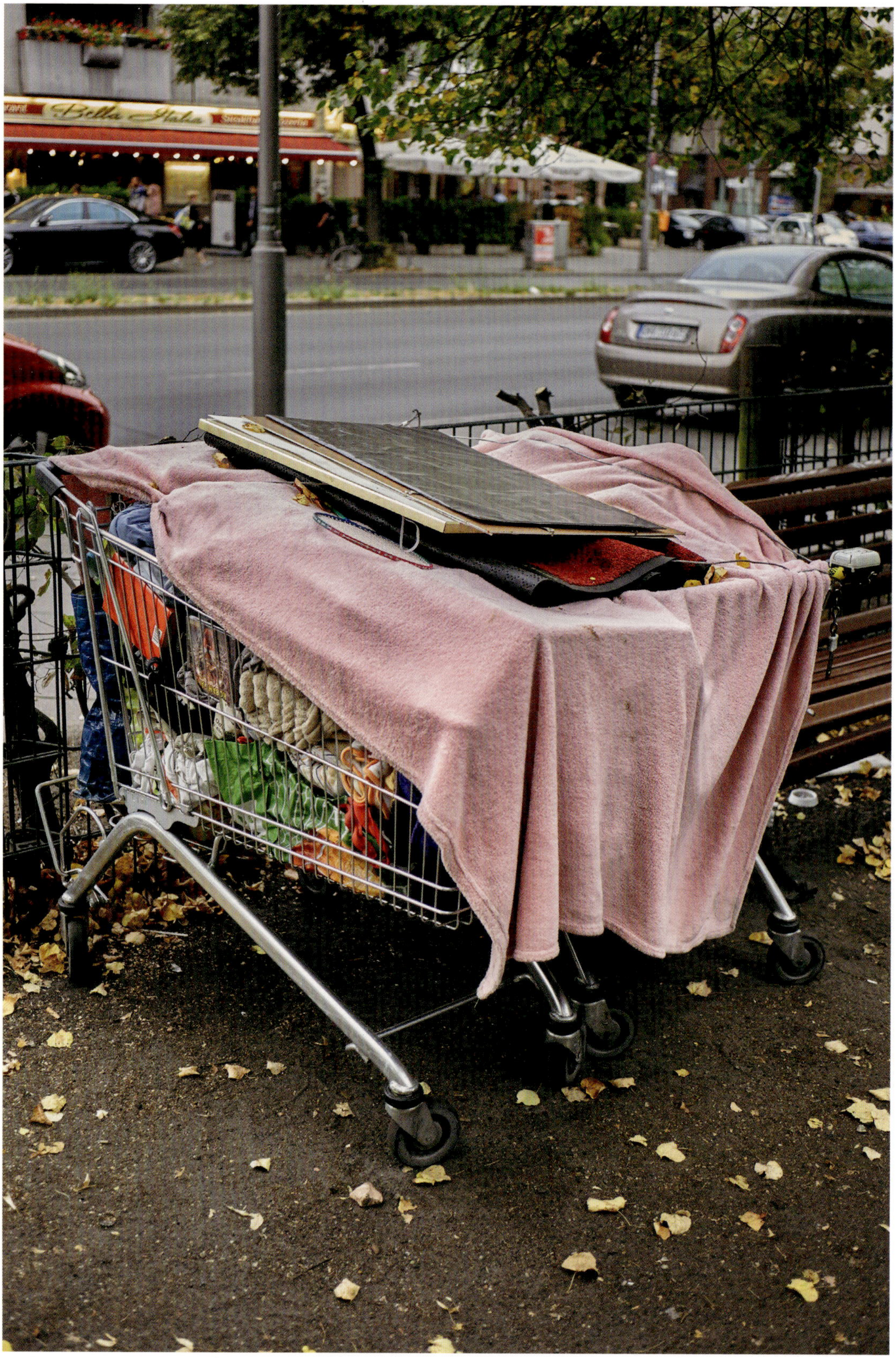

Eine kurze Geschichte des Einkaufswagens

A Short History of the Shopping Cart

Jonathan Progin

Als Sylvan Goldman 1934 die wirtschaftlich schwächelnde Supermarktkette Humpty Dumpty in Oklahoma City übernahm, konnte er nicht wissen, dass er nur zwei Jahre später die Idee seines Lebens haben sollte.[1] Goldman brachte die Kette zwar wieder auf die Erfolgsspur zurück, doch sein größtes Vermächtnis war die Erfindung des Einkaufswagens, einem simplen Gerüst aus Eisen auf vier Rädern, das bald weltweit von Millionen Menschen durch die Gänge zwischen den Supermarktregalen geschoben werden sollte.

In den frühen Dreißigerjahren erholten sich die USA von den Auswirkungen der »Great Depression«, der Wirtschaftskrise, die das Land in eine schwere Rezession stürzte. Gleichzeitig verbreiteten sich die sogenannten Selbstbedienungs-Supermärkte, in denen die Kund*innen eigenständig durch die Gänge gehen und die gewünschten Produkte in Einkaufskörbe legen können, um sie dann an der Kasse zu bezahlen. Dieses Konzept, das mittlerweile Standard ist, stand im krassen Gegensatz zum damals geläufigen Handel über die Theke in Bäckereien oder Metzgereien. Doch trotz einer riesigen Auswahl

When, in 1934, Sylvan Goldman took over the Humpty Dumpty supermarkets in Oklahoma City during the chain's economic decline, he could not have known that in just two years he would have the greatest idea of his life.[1] Though Goldman immediately set the chain on a success course, his major legacy was the invention of the shopping cart, a simple iron structure mounted on four wheels, soon used worldwide, to be pushed through the aisles between supermarket shelves by millions of shoppers.

In the early 1930s, the U.S. was recovering from the effects of the Great Depression that had plunged the country into a major recession. At the same time the so-called self-service supermarket was mushrooming, where customers walked along the aisles on their own and placed the desired articles into their baskets, paying for them later at the cash desk. This now standard concept stood in glaring contrast to the usual custom in bakeries and butchers of the time. Despite a gigantic array of products, customers

[1] Pledger Daugherty, Julia Ann: »Goldman, Sylvan Nathan (1898–1984)«, in: Oklahoma History Society: *The Encyclopedia of Oklahoma History and Culture*, o. D. n. d., online verfügbar unter available online at: https://www.okhistory.org/publications/enc/entry.php?entry=GO004 [zuletzt abgerufen am last accessed 20.06.2020].

an unterschiedlichsten Produkten hatten Supermärkte ein Problem: Kund*innen kauften nur so viel ein, wie in den Körben Platz hatte.

Für Sylvan Goldman war klar: Eine Lösung musste her. Die Idee für den Einkaufswagen kam ihm eines Abends im Jahr 1936 beim Anblick von zwei Klappstühlen in seinem Büro.[2] Er begriff, dass größere Einkaufskörbe zu schwer zu tragen wären – also mussten sie nicht getragen, sondern geschoben werden. Goldman beauftragte den in einem seiner Läden angestellten Mechaniker Fred Young mit der Umsetzung dieser Idee. Schnell stellten sich kleinere Probleme ein, die nicht einer gewissen Komik entbehren: Die ersten Prototypen neigten dazu, sofort zusammenzuklappen, wenn die Räder an etwas stießen, oder umzukippen, wenn sie um eine Kurve geschoben wurden.[3] Doch Young behob alle Mängel und flickte für Goldman den ersten funktionierenden Einkaufswagen (»shopping cart«) der Welt zusammen. Allerdings war dieses Gefährt eher ein Klappstuhl mit Rädern und Ablagen, in die man übereinander zwei Einkaufskörbe hineinlegen konnte, als ein wirklicher Wagen.[4]

could only buy as much as they could fit into their shopping bags or baskets.

It became clear to Sylvan Goldman that he had to find a solution. The idea of a shopping cart came to him one evening in 1936 when he noticed two folding chairs in his office.[2] He understood that larger bags would be too heavy, that they needed to be pushed rather than carried around the store. He commissioned Fred Young, his own hired mechanic, to implement this idea. Small problems didn't take long to turn up, often with a touch of comic relief. The first prototypes tended to fold up when the wheels hit something or were shoved around a curve.[3] But Young quickly got rid of all the defects and he cobbled together for Goldman the first functional shopping cart in the world, although the contraption was more like a folding chair with wheels and a tray onto which two shopping baskets could be placed, one above the other, than a real wagon.[4] The lower chassis, with its legs crossed like an X,

[2] Grandclément, Catherine: »Wheeling One's Groceries Around the Store: The Invention of the Shopping Cart, 1936–1953«, in: Belasco, Warren / Horowitz, Roger (Hg. eds.): *Food Chains: From Farmyard to Shopping Cart*, Philadelphia 2009, S. pp. 233–251, hier S. p. 235.
[3] Ebd. Ibid., S. p. 235.
[4] Ebd. Ibid., S. p. 236.

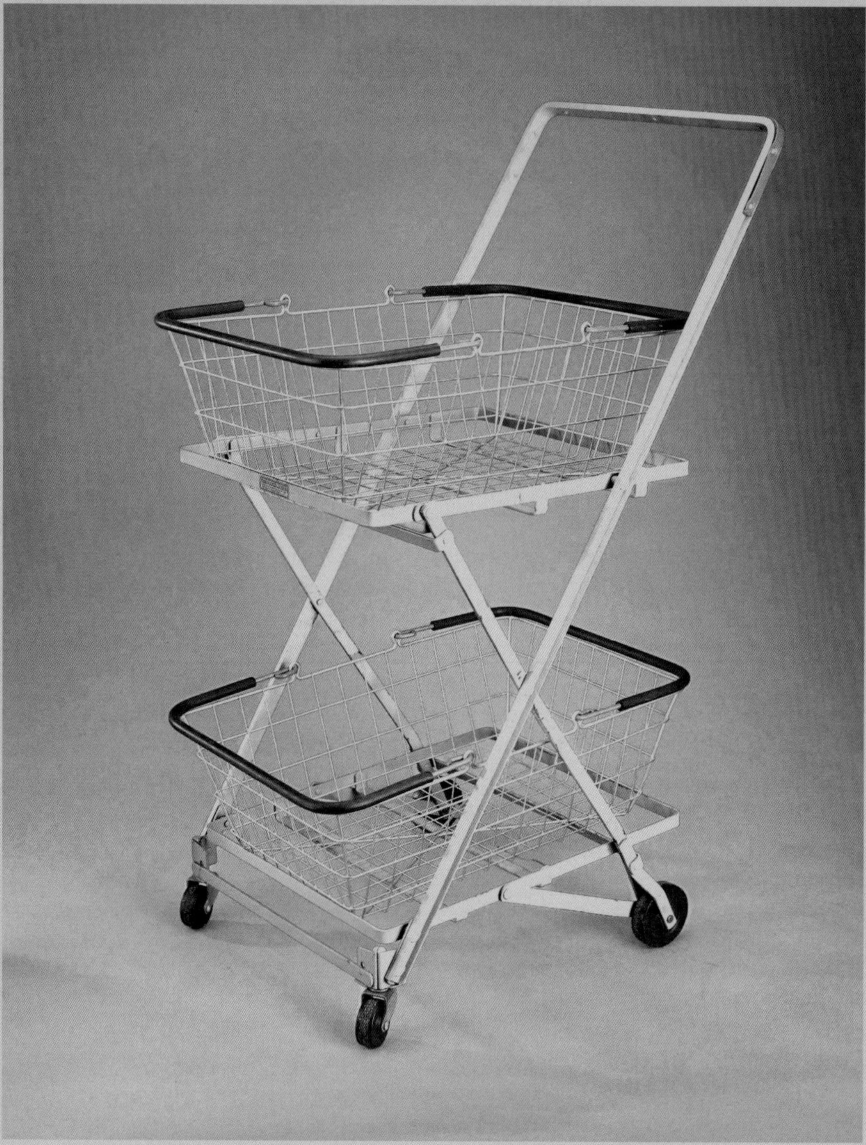

Der erste Einkaufswagen von Sylvan Goldman, circa 1937
The first shopping cart by Sylvan Goldman, circa 1937

Quelle Source

Division of Work and Industry, National Museum of American History, Smithsonian Institution, Washington, D.C.

Das unten angebrachte Fahrgestell mit seinen zwei »Standbeinen«, die wie ein X verstrebt waren, erinnerte entfernt an einen Wäscheständer. Trotz der vermeintlichen Lösung des Problems war das Modell zu Beginn alles andere als ein Erfolg.

Am 4. Juni 1937 veröffentlichte Goldman in Lokalzeitungen Werbeanzeigen für den Humpty-Dumpty-Supermarkt mit der Abbildung einer Frau, die ihren vollbeladenen Einkaufskorb fast nicht mehr tragen konnte. »It's new – it's sensational. No more baskets to carry«, stand dazu in großen Lettern geschrieben, mehr nicht.[5] Wer also wissen wollte, was sich hinter dieser kryptischen Nachricht verbarg, musste einen entsprechenden Supermarkt aufsuchen. Doch die vom Zeitungsinserat angelockten Kund*innen waren alles andere als begeistert, als sie dieses Klappergestell sahen. Während Männer sich für stark genug hielten, um die Körbe durch den Laden zu tragen, sagten Frauen, sie hätten schon genug Kinderwagen geschoben.[6] Eine andere Strategie musste also her, um die Einkaufswagen populär zu machen. Goldman beauftragte daraufhin Schauspieler*innen und seine eige-

vaguely resembled a clothes horse. Despite the presumed solution to the problem, this model began as anything but a success.

On June 4, 1937, Goldman took out ads in local papers for the Humpty Dumpty supermarket that depicted customers who could hardly carry their piled-high shopping baskets. »It's new—it's sensational. No more baskets to carry,« proclaimed the ad in large letters.[5] Anyone who wanted to know what this cryptic message was about had to head for a relevant store. But the customers who did were not at all enthused by the rickety frameworks they saw there. Men found they were strong enough to carry the baskets through the store themselves, while the women said thank you, they had already pushed enough baby carriages to last them a lifetime.[6] A different strategy was needed to popularize the cart. Goldman sent out both actors and his own employees to walk through the markets with loaded wagons. As customers began to get used to the sight, they slowly followed suit. Goldman

[5] Ebd. Ibid., S. p. 235 f.
[6] Ebd. Ibid., S. p. 237.

nen Angestellten, mit den Einkaufswagen zwischen den Regalen in seinen Läden herumzugehen. Die Kund*innen gewöhnten sich schnell an diesen Anblick und übernahmen fortan die Praxis, beim Einkaufen die Produkte in den Wagen zu legen. Goldman ließ seine Erfindung patentieren und durch sein Unternehmen, die Folding Carrier Basket Company, produzieren.[7]

Aber eine wichtige Komponente fehlte den Wagen noch, damit sie zu den »shopping carts« werden konnten, wie wir sie heute in fast allen Supermärkten vorfinden: die hintere Schwingtüre, mit denen sich die einzelnen Modelle ineinanderschieben lassen. Diese simple Vorrichtung war allerdings nicht die Idee von Sylvan Goldman, sondern von Orla E. Watson, einem Zeichner und Schlosser aus Kansas City. Eines Tages im Frühjahr 1946, kurz nach dem Zweiten Weltkrieg, war er unterwegs, um seine Einkäufe zu tätigen, und konnte beobachten, wie viel Raum die herumstehenden Einkaufswagen vor den Läden einnahmen.[8] Also begann er zu tüfteln und kam schließlich auf die Lösung des Problems: feste Gestelle mit einer hinten angebrachten

had his invention patented, and it was produced by a company named the Folding Carrier Basket Company.[7]

But there was an important component still missing before the invention would become the shopping carts we know today and find in almost every supermarket in the world: namely folding doors at the back of the wire baskets allowing individual carts to be shoved together. This simple concept was not Sylvan Goldman's idea but that of Orla E. Watson, a draughtsman and mechanic from Kansas City. One day in the spring of 1946, Watson was on his way to go shopping when he noticed how much room the many empty wagons took up parked in front of the store.[8] He began experimenting with various ideas and finally arrived at a solution: solid frameworks with a back-end folding door, the so-called »telescoping shopping cart.«

In October 1947, however, only one-and-a-half years after Watson's shopping experiment,

[7] Pledger Daugherty, 2009, o. D. n. d.
[8] Grandclément, 2009, S. p. 242.

Schwingtür, sogenannte »telescoping shopping carts«.

Doch im Oktober 1947, nur anderthalb Jahre nach Watsons Einkaufserlebnis, stellte plötzlich das Unternehmen von Goldman ein neuartiges Wagenmodell mit dem kuriosen Namen »New Triple-Plus Capacity Nest-Baskart« vor.[9] Diese Neuheit hatte einen einzigen großen Korb und ein überraschend ähnliches Schwingtürsystem wie das von Watson. Was dann folgte, war ein jahrelanger Rechtsstreit um Patente und Prestige, den schließlich der viel reichere Goldman gewann. Er musste lediglich einen symbolischen Dollar an Watson überweisen, um die exklusiven Rechte zu erhalten, einen Einkaufswagen mit Schwingtüre verkaufen zu dürfen.[10]

Und so begann der Einkaufswagen – ausgestattet mit einem stabilen Fahrgestell, einem großzügigen Korb und einer Schwingtüre – seinen weltweiten Siegeszug. Im Nachkriegseuropa der Fünfzigerjahre kam der Gitterwagen aus den USA gerade richtig: Die westeuropäische Wirtschaft boomte und die Menschen entdeckten die Lust am Massenkonsum –

Goldman presented a new »Triple-Plus Capacity Nest-Baskart.«[9] This innovation had a single large basket and a back-end folding door system surprisingly similar to Watson's. What followed was a year-long legal battle centered on patents and prestige, which the financially richer Goldman finally won. He needed only to wire a symbolic dollar to Watson in order to have the exclusive right to sell the shopping cart with folding backdoor inserts.[10]

Thus the shopping cart—equipped with a stable framework, a large basket, and a push-in back—began its worldwide victory march. The metal mesh wagon from the U.S. arrived at the right moment in Europe. The West European economy was booming and its residents discovered their lust for mass consumption. Meanwhile the practical shopping cart in the new supermarkets had never made consumption so simple. In Germany the first carts arrived in 1951[11], in Switzerland several years later[12]. In time other cart models appeared, with drag chains and

[9] Ebd. Ibid., S. p. 245.
[10] Ebd. Ibid., S. p. 246.

und mit dem praktischen Einkaufswagen in den neuen Supermärkten war das Konsumieren so einfach wie nie zuvor. In Deutschland fuhren die »shopping carts« erstmals 1951[11] zwischen den Regalen, in der Schweiz ein paar Jahre später[12]. Mit der Zeit folgten dann Modelle mit Sperrketten und Münzeinwurf, Kindersitzen oder Werbeflächen.[13] Regelrechte Hochkonjunktur hatten die Wagen dann in den riesigen Einkaufszentren, die sich zuerst in den Vorstädten großer US-Metropolen breitmachten und dann in den Sechzigerjahren auch in Europa errichtet wurden. Damals herrschte noch das Ideal der sogenannten »autogerechten Stadt«, also einer Stadt, deren Planung sich am Individualverkehr ausrichtet. So entstanden beispielsweise in den Agglomerationen von Berlin, Frankfurt, München, Wien oder Zürich riesige Konsumtempel, die schnell mit dem Auto erreichbar waren. Und so konnten die Menschen ganz einfach zuerst den Einkaufswagen und dann den Kofferraum mit allen erdenklichen Waren füllen.

Doch mit dem rasanten Aufstieg des Einkaufs im Internet begann der

coin slots, kids' seats or advertisements.[13] The carts then had an absolute boom in the gigantic shopping centers, temples of consumption that were built in the suburbs of large metropolises such as Berlin, Frankfurt, Munich, Vienna, and Zurich, and were able to be quickly reached by car. People could fill first their shopping carts and then the trunks of their cars with every imaginable sort of product.

Yet more recently, with the rapid rise in Internet shopping, a gradual decline in shopping carts has inevitably followed. The carts still stand at the entrances to supermarkets and are still in use, but with the spread of online orders they are becoming ever more insignificant. When the courier replaces the shopping cart, a metal wagon on wheels has become redundant. In the meantime, it is not rare for goods such as toilet paper or even fresh veggies to be ordered from the Net. Yet even with »same day delivery« the shopping cart is never far away, for, in almost all online shops,

[11] Hauffe, Thomas: *Geschichte des Designs*, Köln Cologne 2014, S. p. 168.
[12] Feusi, Alois: »Einkaufswagen«, in: Schneeberger, Paul (Hg. ed.): *Schweizer Mobiliar*, Zürich Zurich 2010, S. pp. 29–32, hier S. p. 30.
[13] Hauffe, 2014, S. p. 168.

schleichende Abstieg der Einkaufswagen. Zwar stehen sie immer noch vor den Eingängen der Supermärkte und werden nach wie vor benutzt, aber mit der weiteren Verbreitung von Online-Shops geraten sie immer stärker in die Bedeutungslosigkeit. Wenn der Paketdienst zum Einkaufswagen wird, braucht man das Eisengestell auf Rädern nicht mehr. Mittlerweile ist es auch keine Seltenheit, dass Gemüse oder Toilettenpapier im Internet bestellt werden. Aber in Vergessenheit geraten wird der Einkaufswagen trotz »same day delivery« nicht. Denn in fast allen Online-Shops wird Goldmans Erfindung als virtuelles Symbol für den Einkauf selbst prominent hervorgehoben. Bevor Kund*innen ihre Bestellung abschließen können, müssen sie den digitalen Einkaufswagen erst zur Kasse führen und ihren Einkauf bezahlen. Und so wurde aus dem ursprünglichen Korb auf Rädern das Symbol für den Konsum schlechthin, das überall auf der Welt verstanden wird.

Jonathan Progin, geboren 1995, ist ein Schweizer Journalist. Er hat Politikwissenschaft und Geschichte der Neuzeit an der Universität Zürich studiert. Progin lebt und arbeitet in Zürich.

Goldman's invention is prominently highlighted as a symbol for the act of purchasing itself. Before customers can finalize their order, they must tap a symbolic digital shopping cart in order to pay at the online checkout. Thus the original wheeled wagon has become a symbol of consumption per se, which is accepted as such all around the world.

Jonathan Progin, born 1995, is a Swiss journalist. He studied political science and modern history at the University of Zurich. Progin lives and works in Zurich.

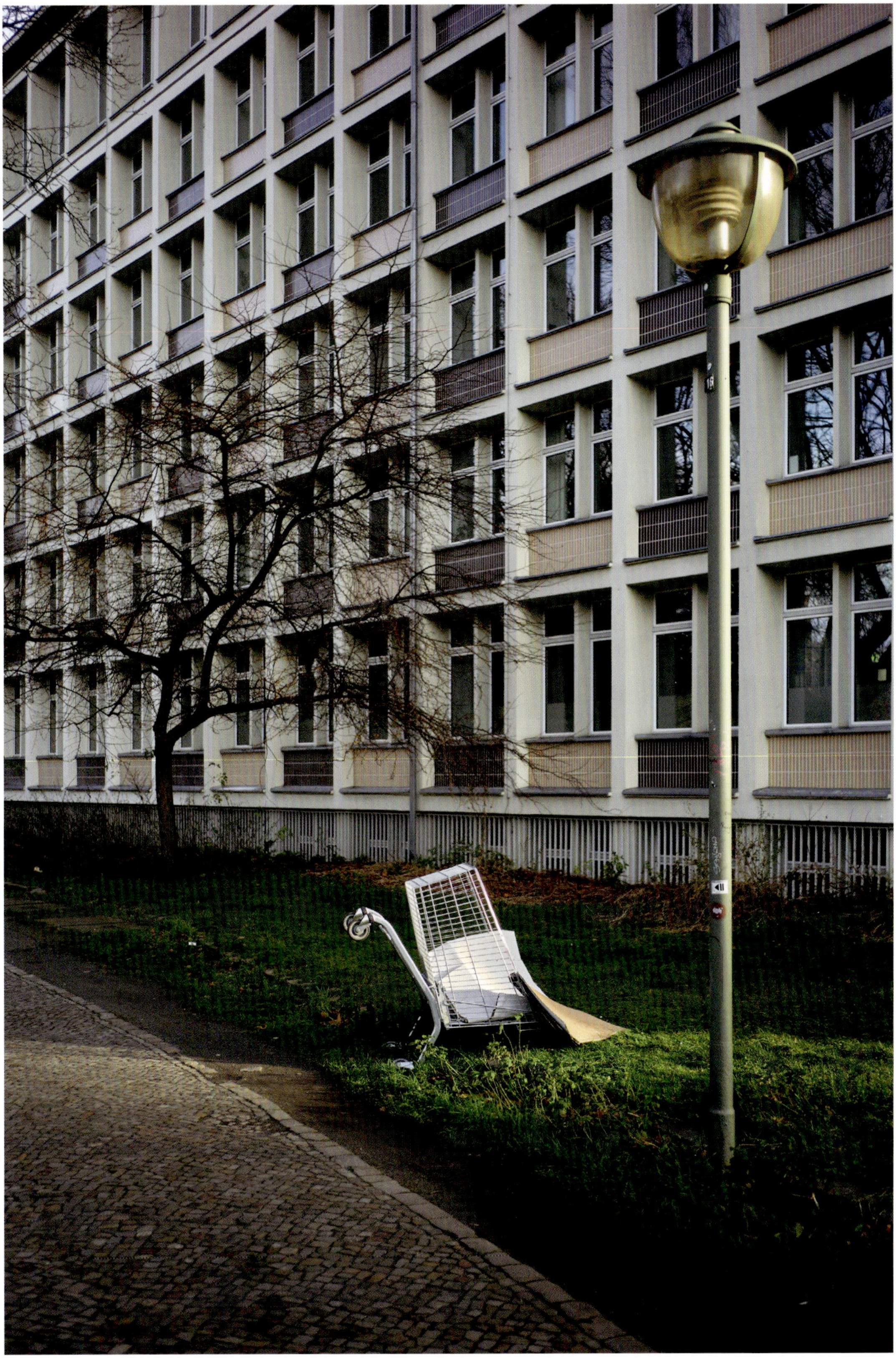

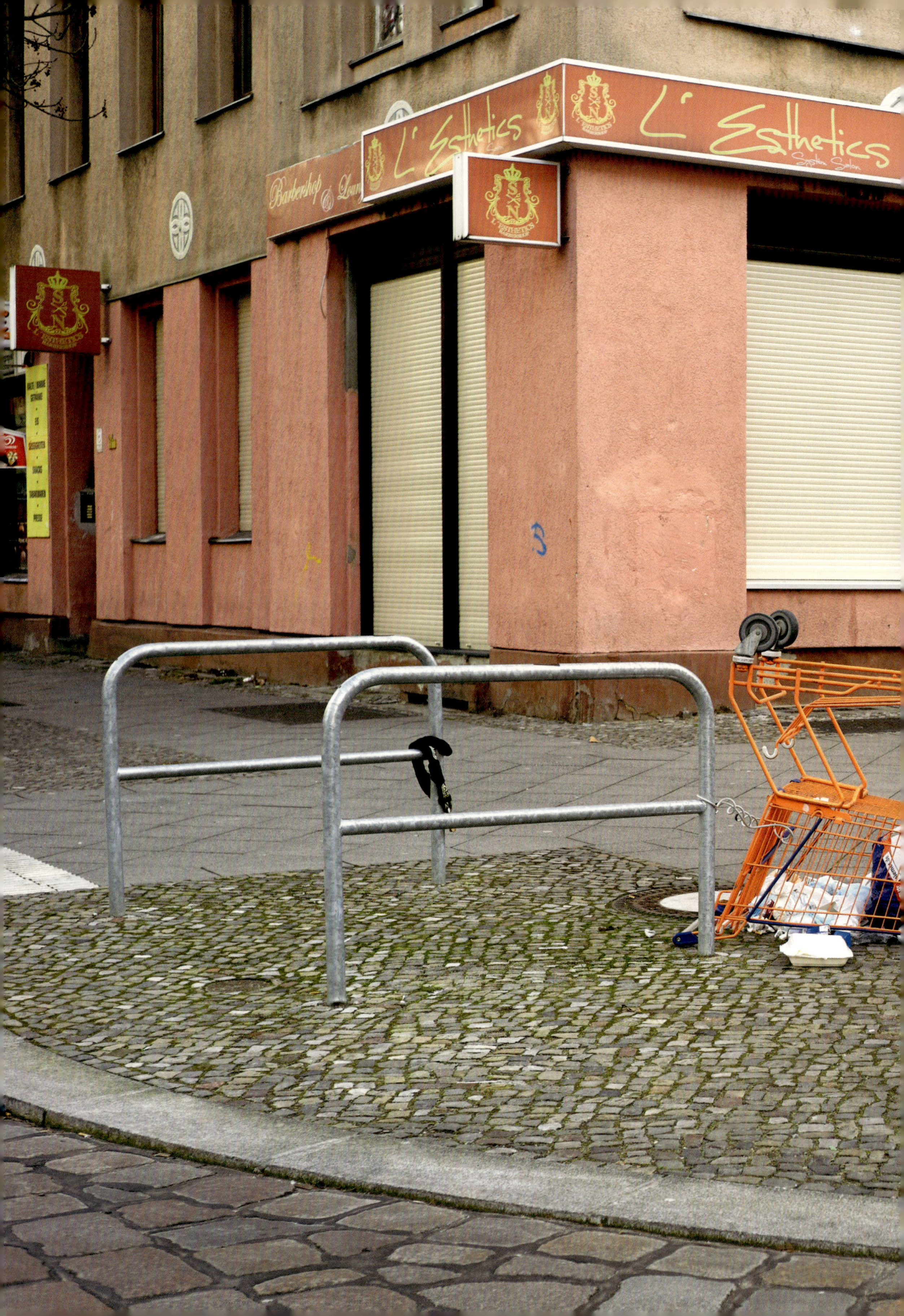
L' Esthetics
L' Esthetics
Barbershop

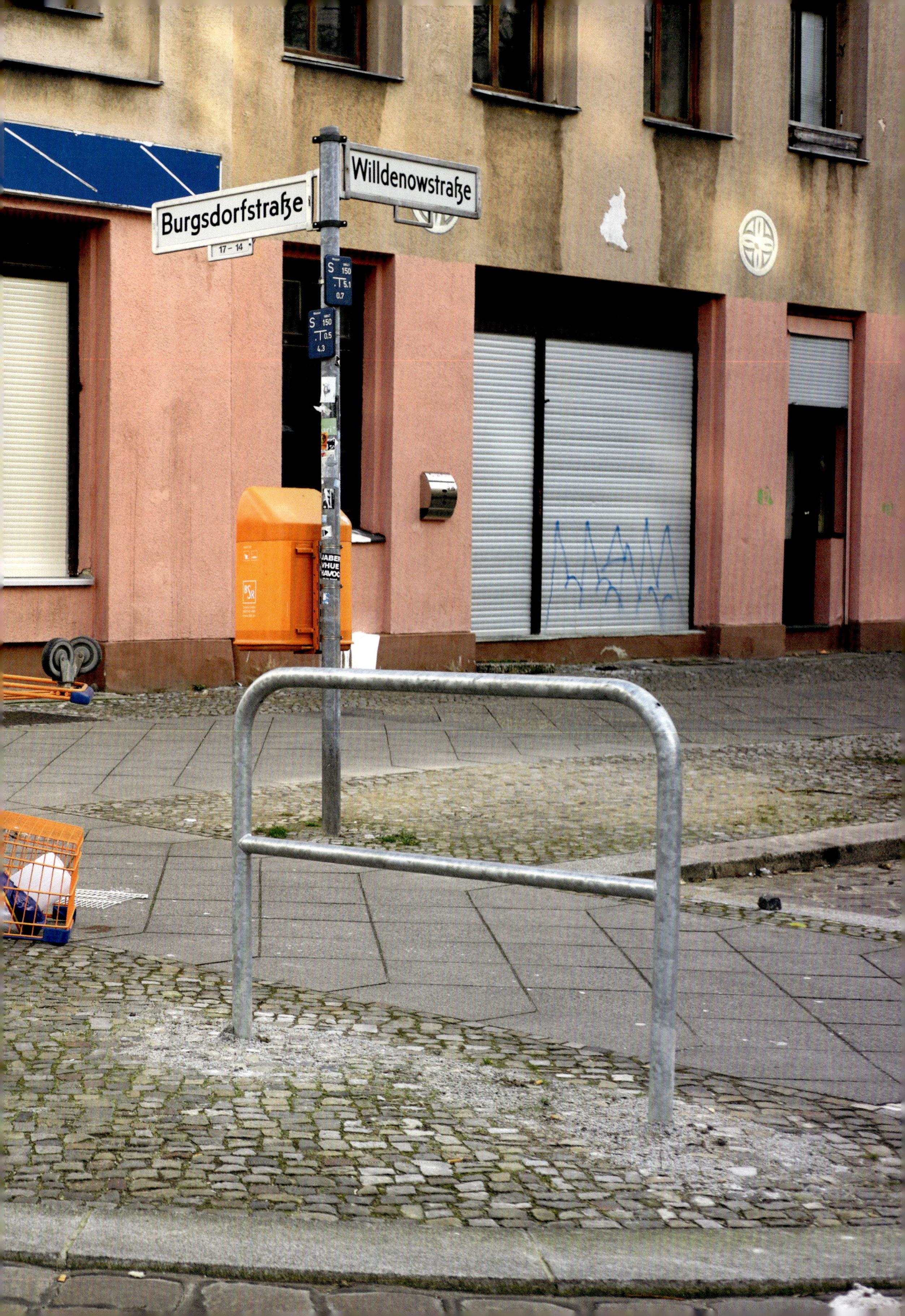
Burgsdorfstraße
17 – 14
Willdenowstraße

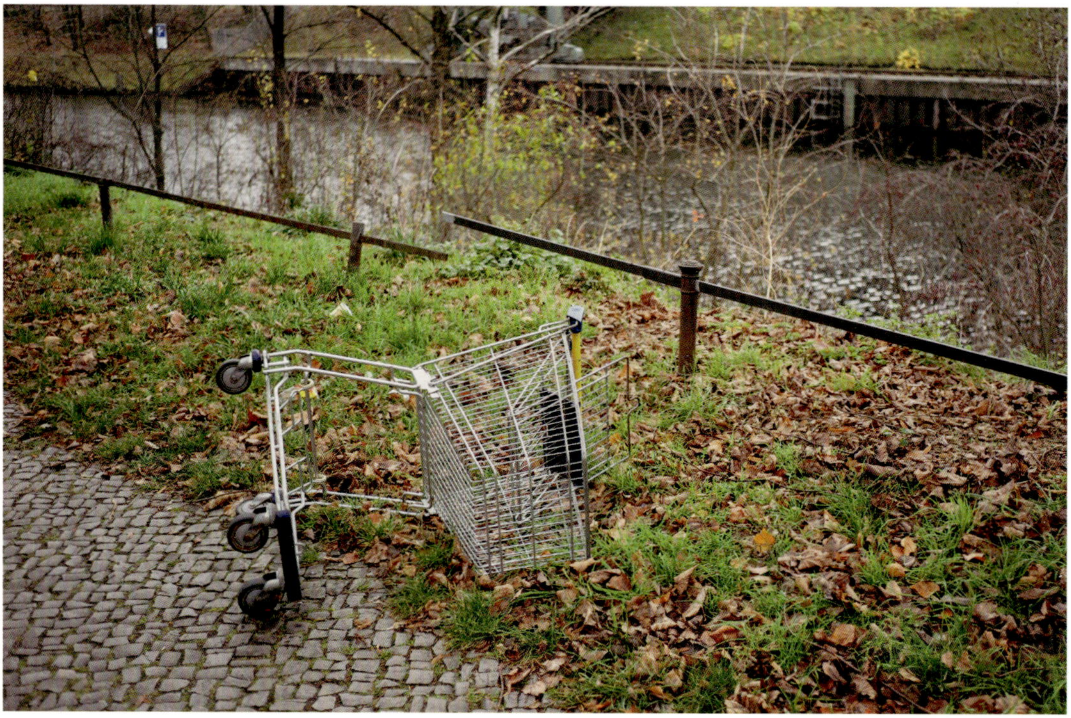

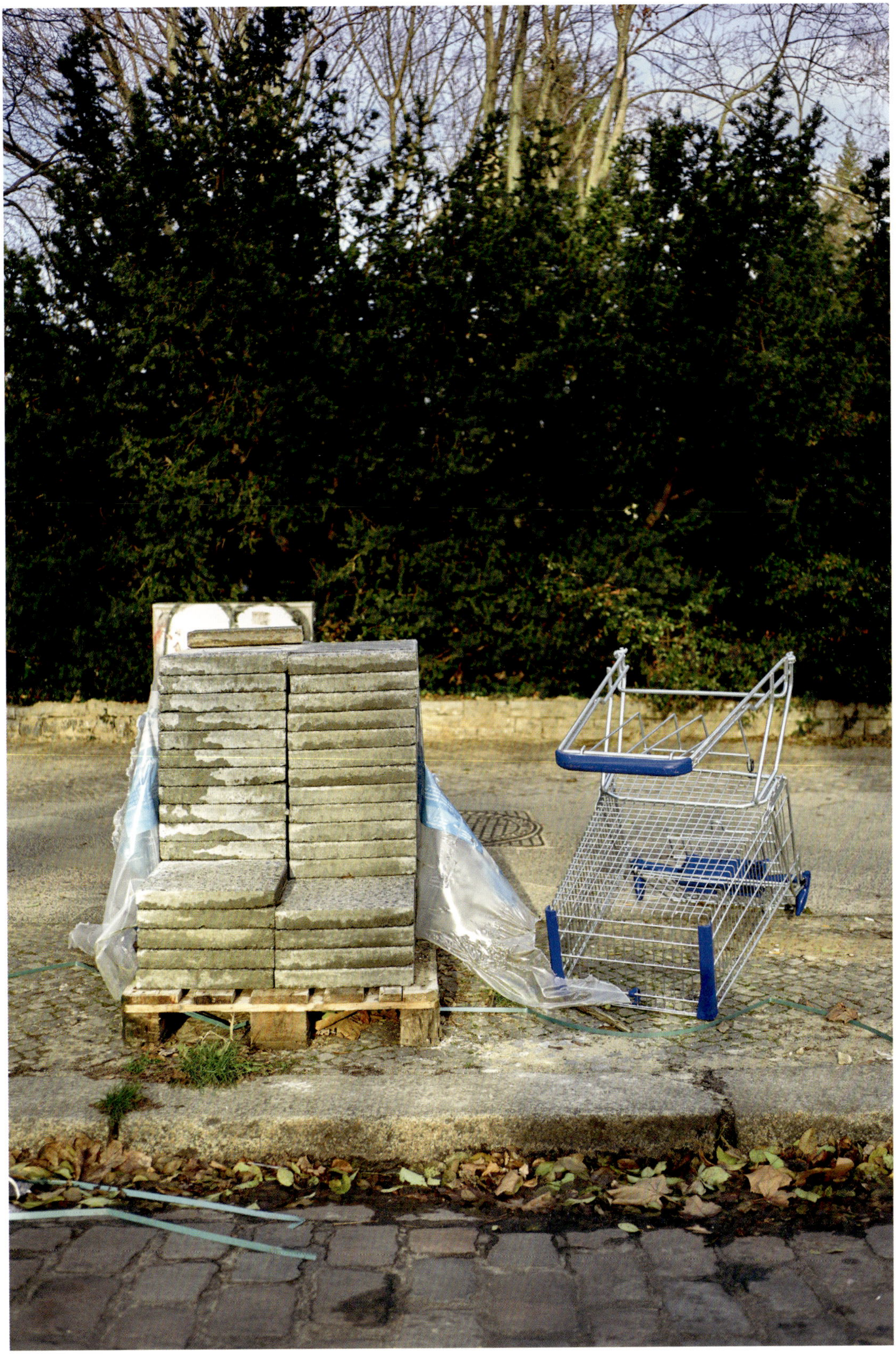

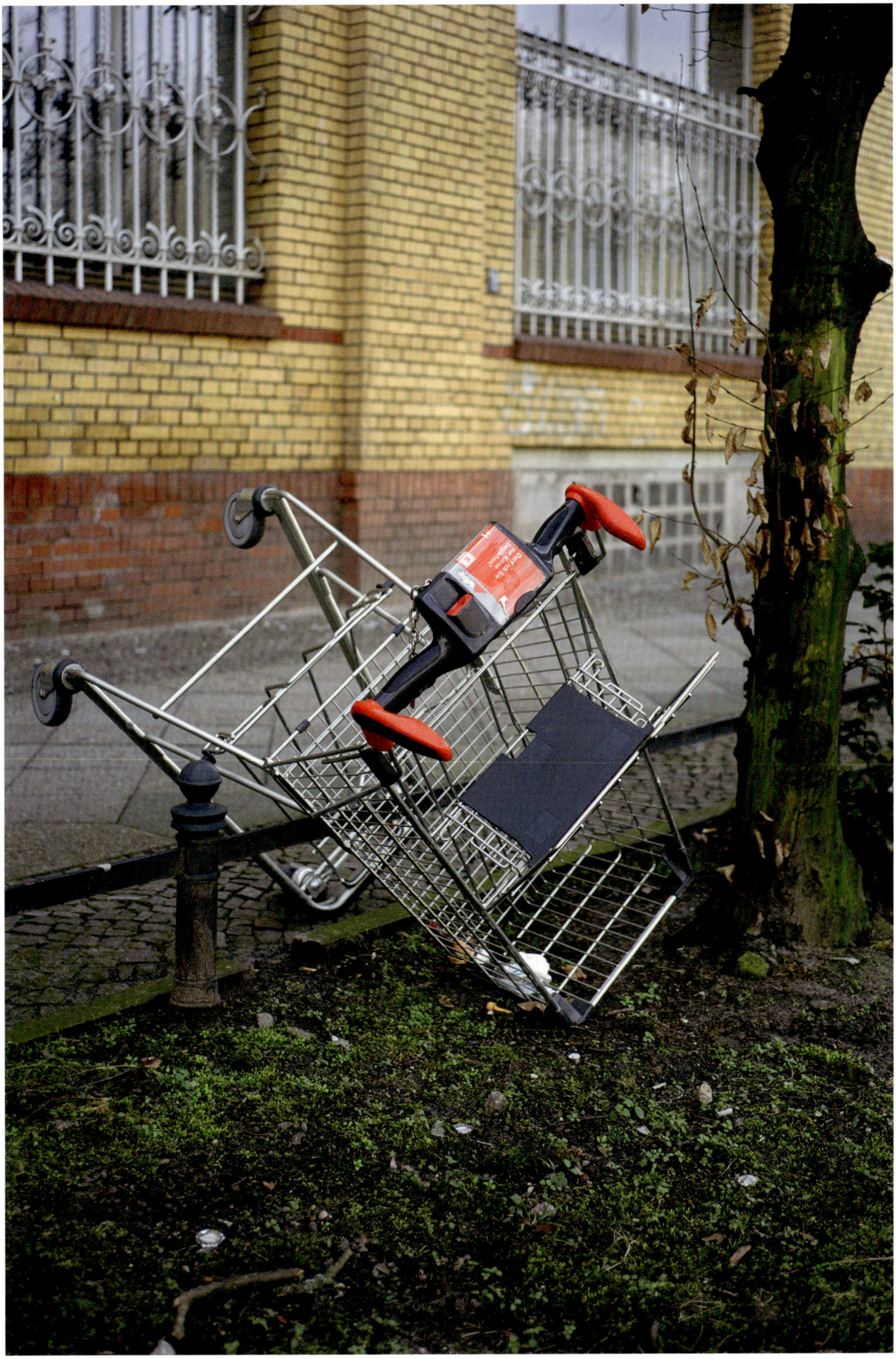

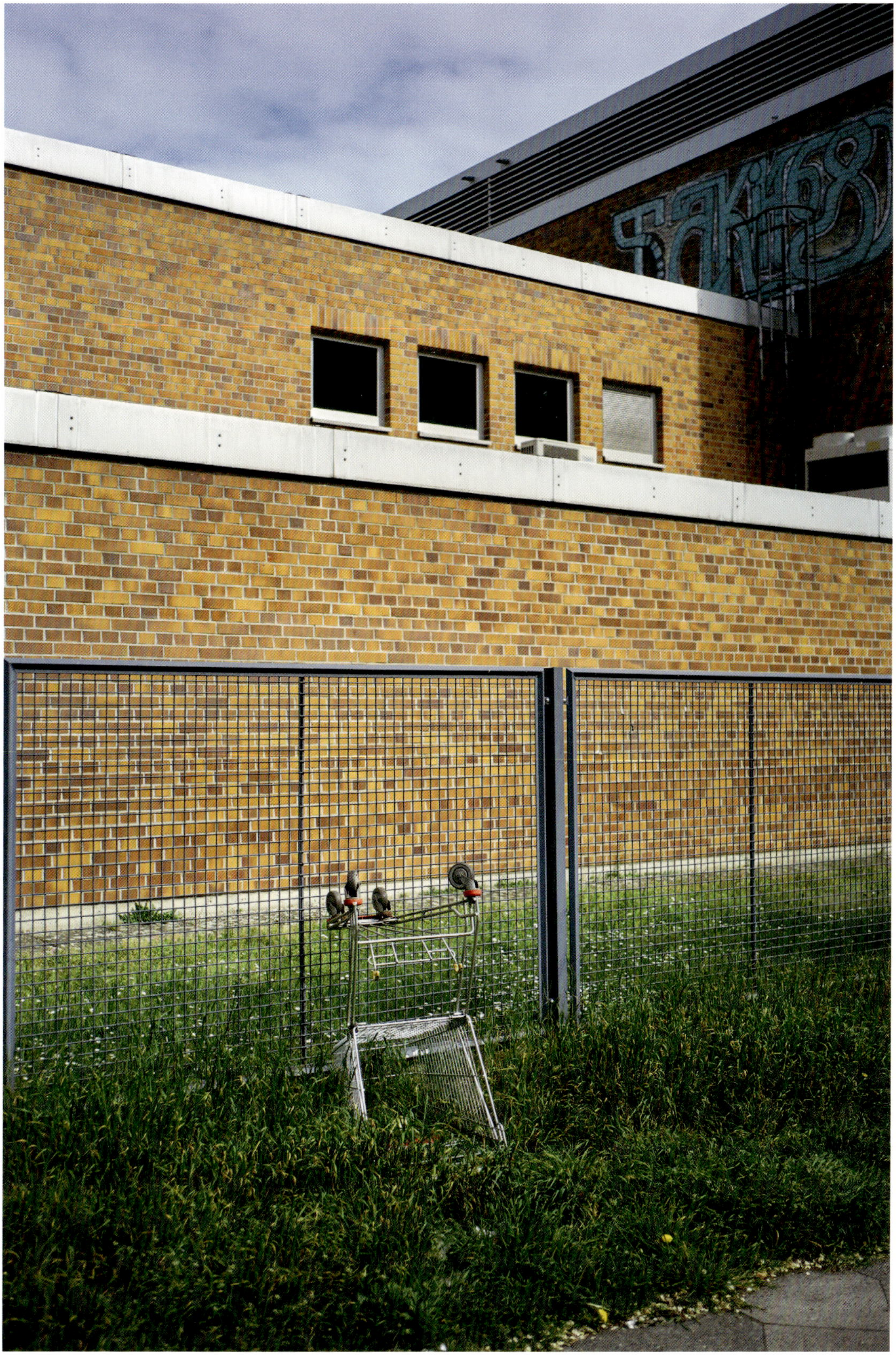

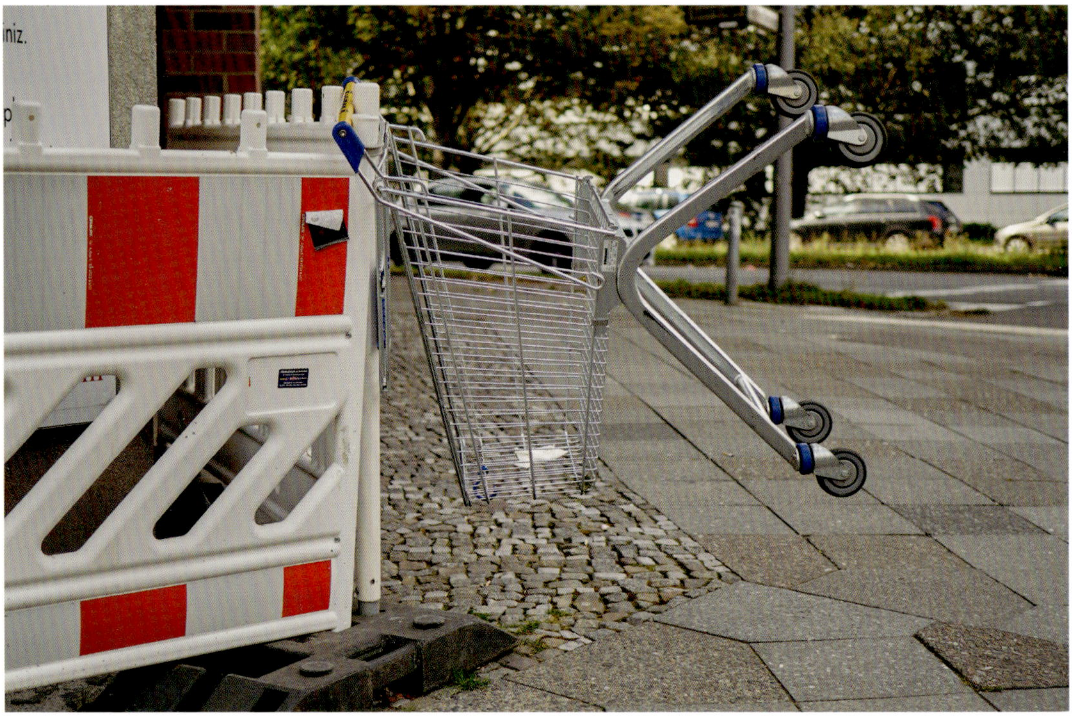

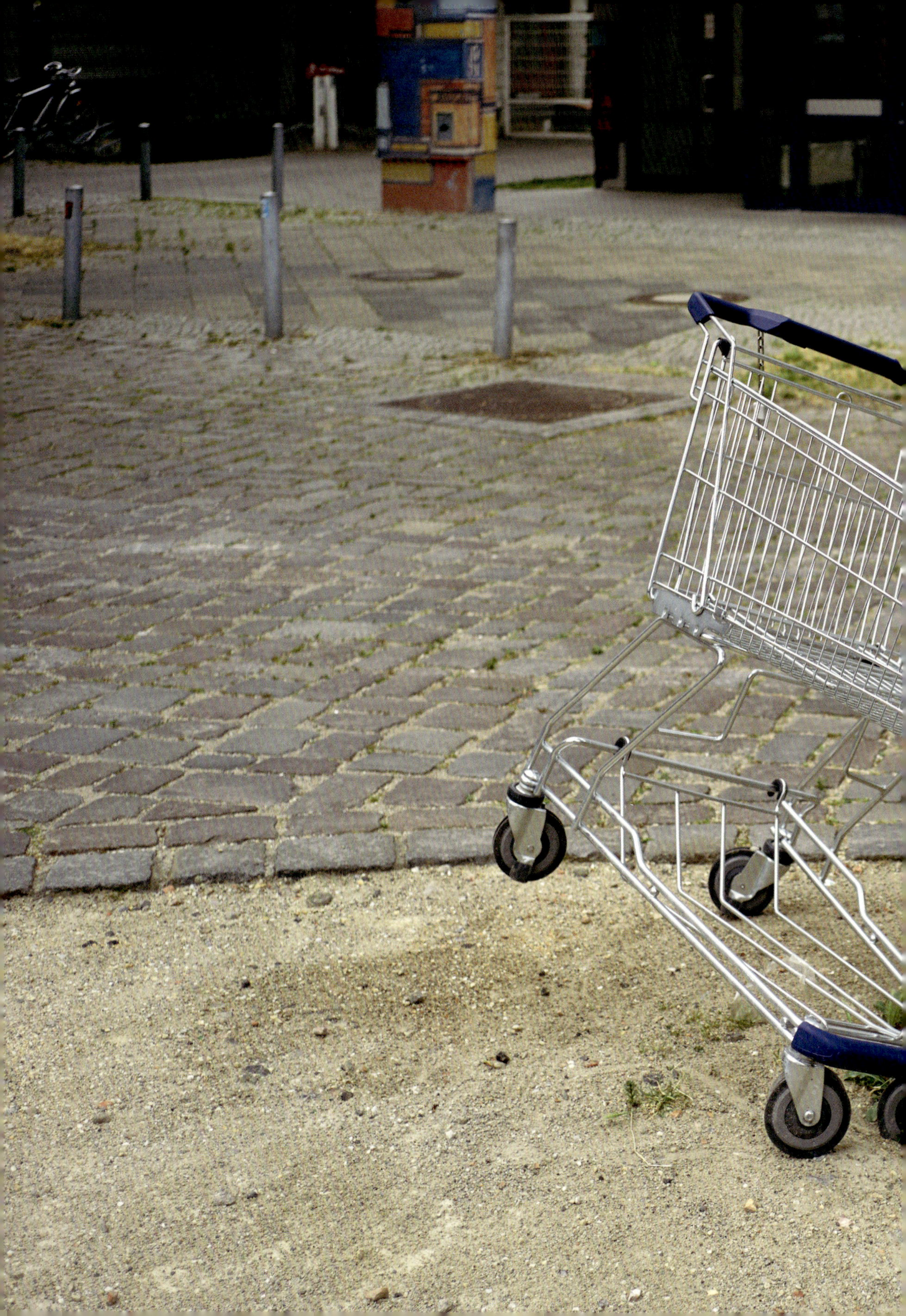

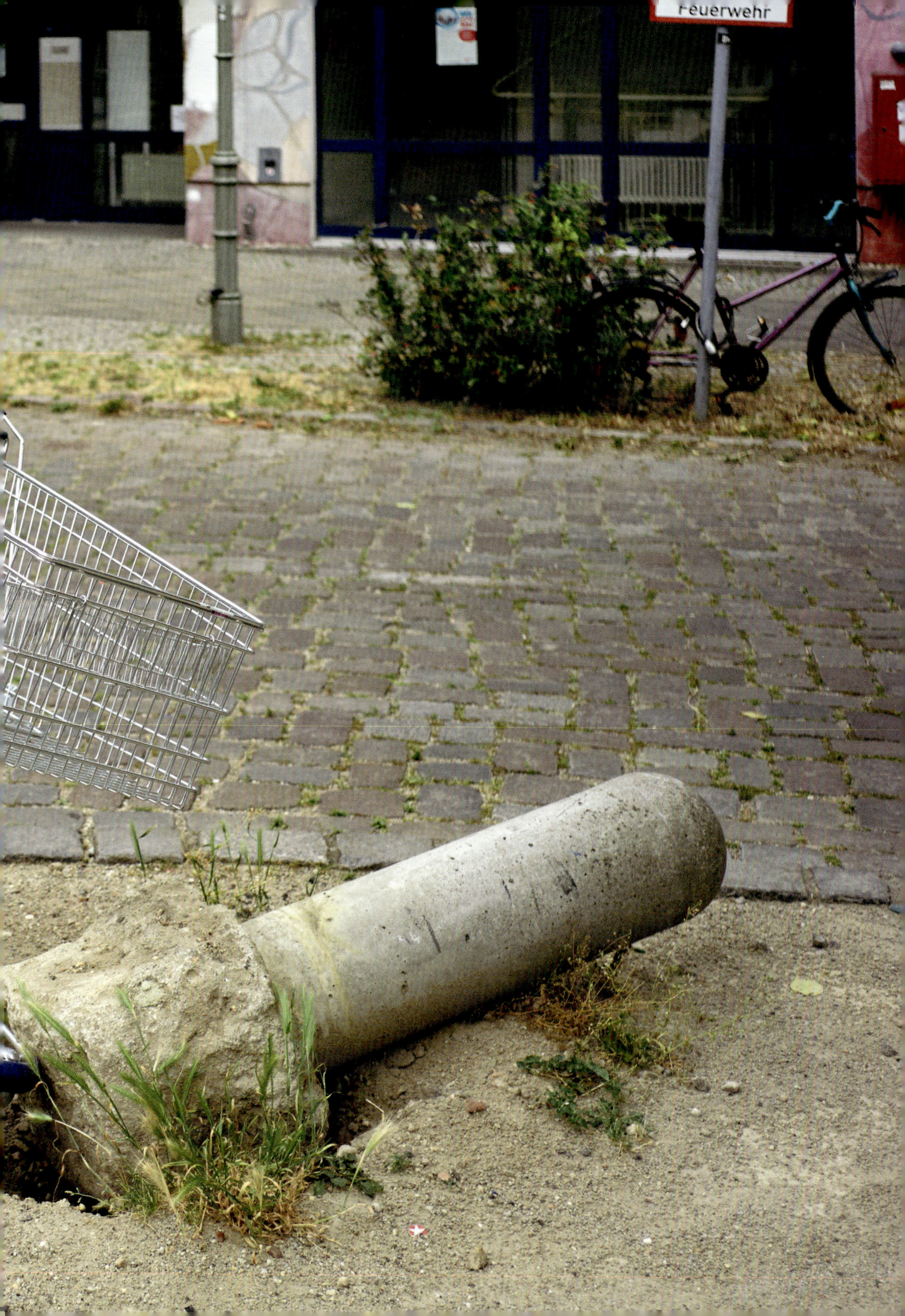
Feuerwehr

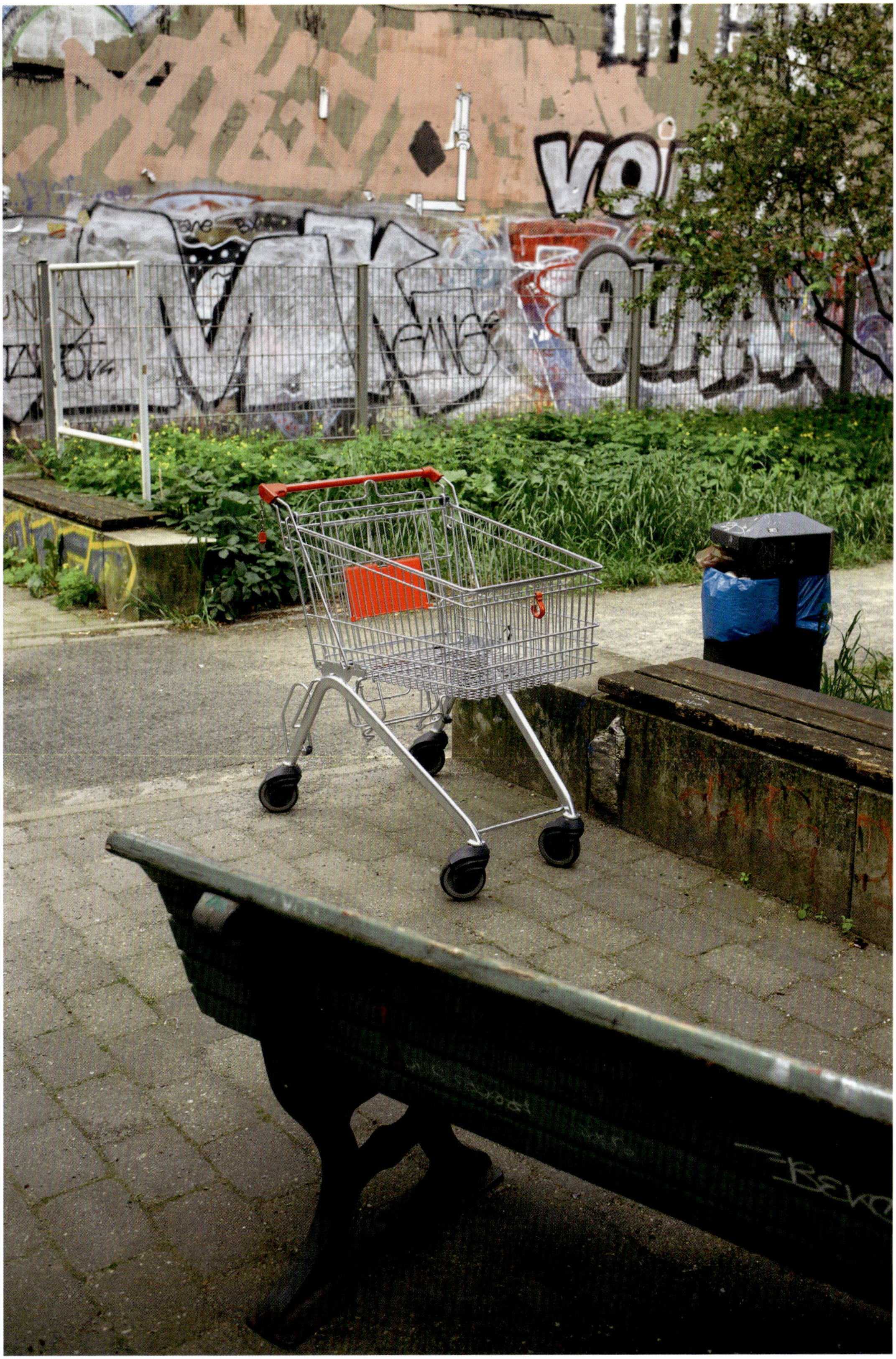

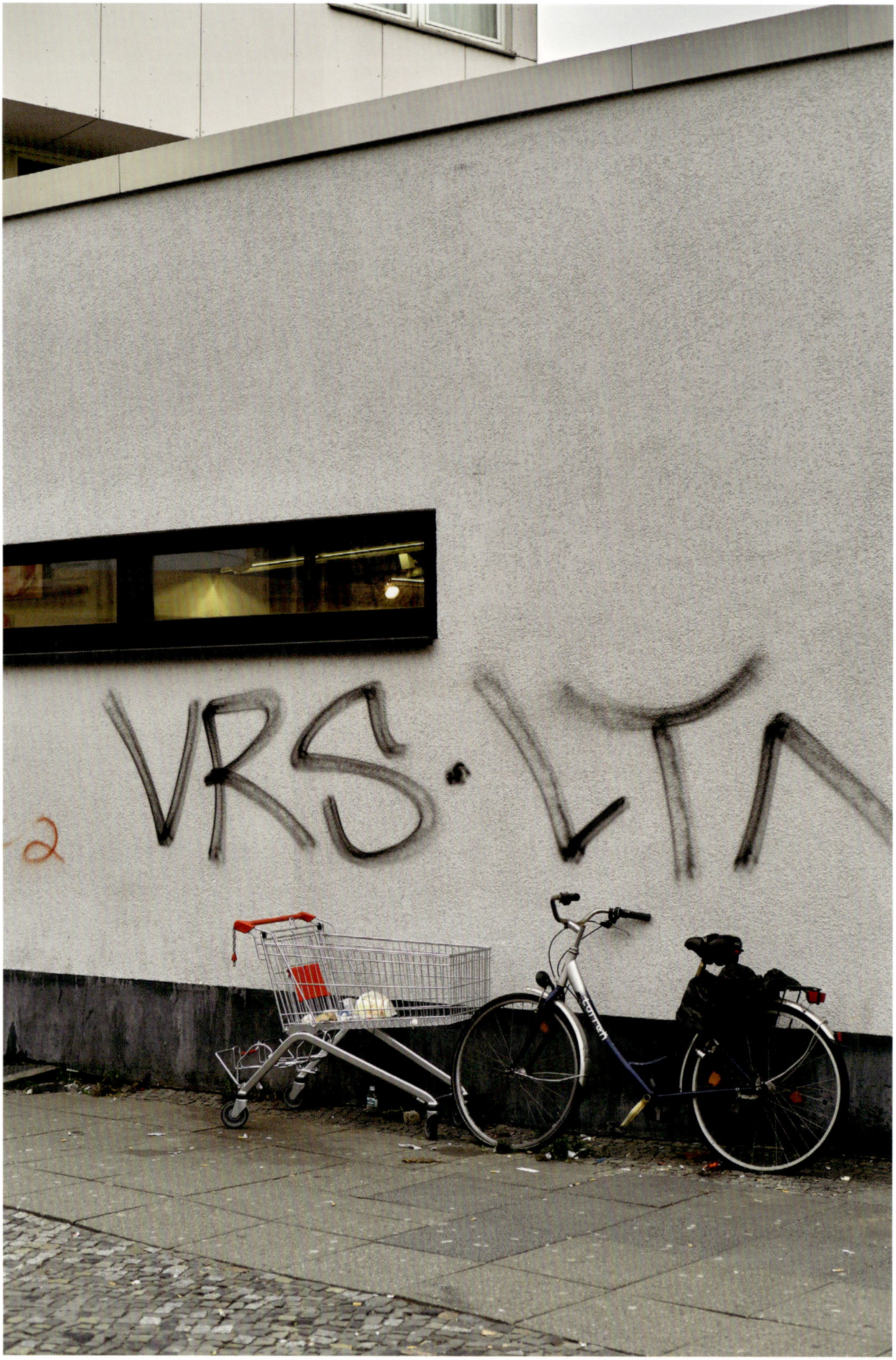

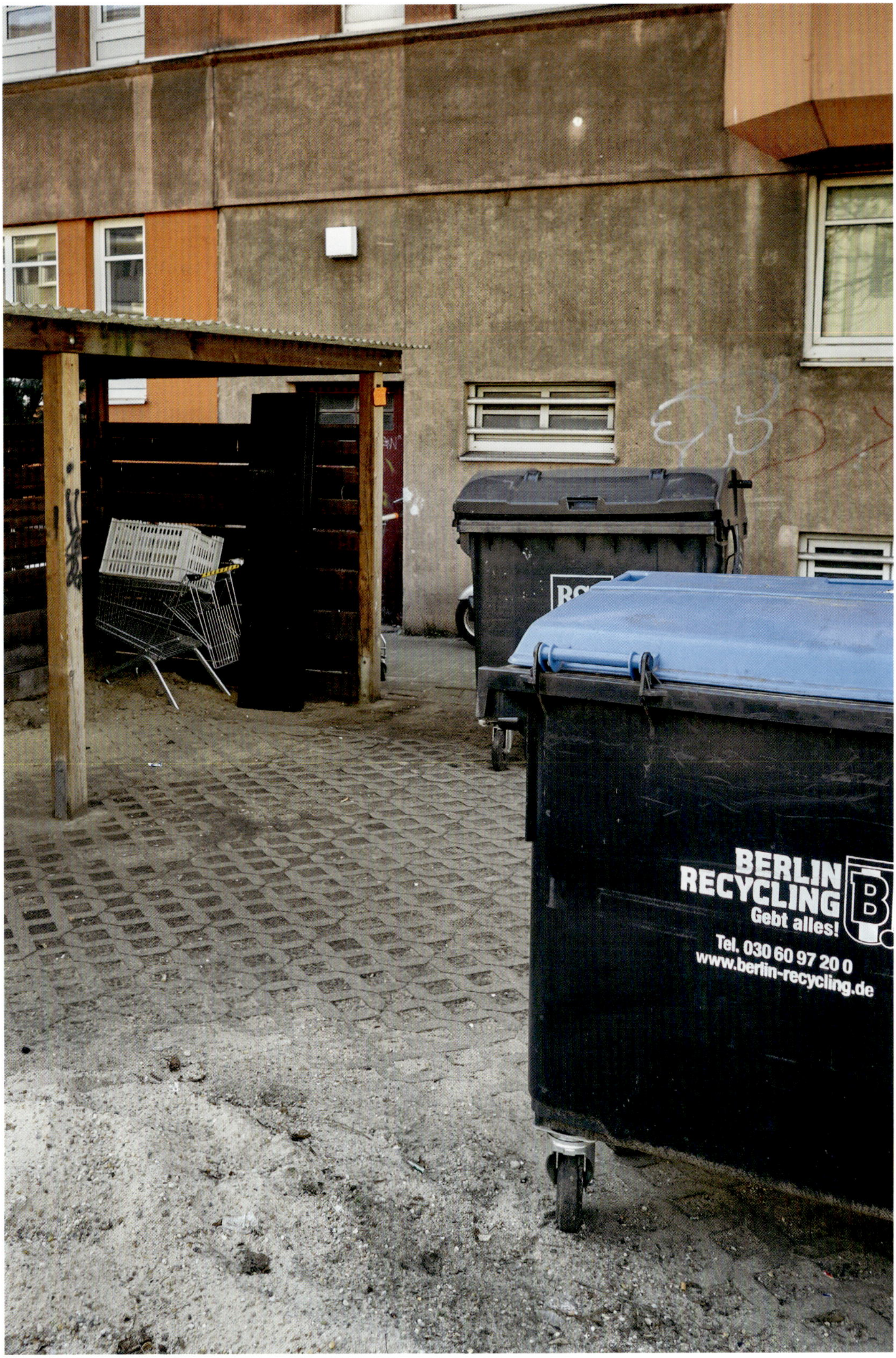
BERLIN
RECYCLING
Gebt alles!
Tel. 030 60 97 20 0
www.berlin-recycling.de

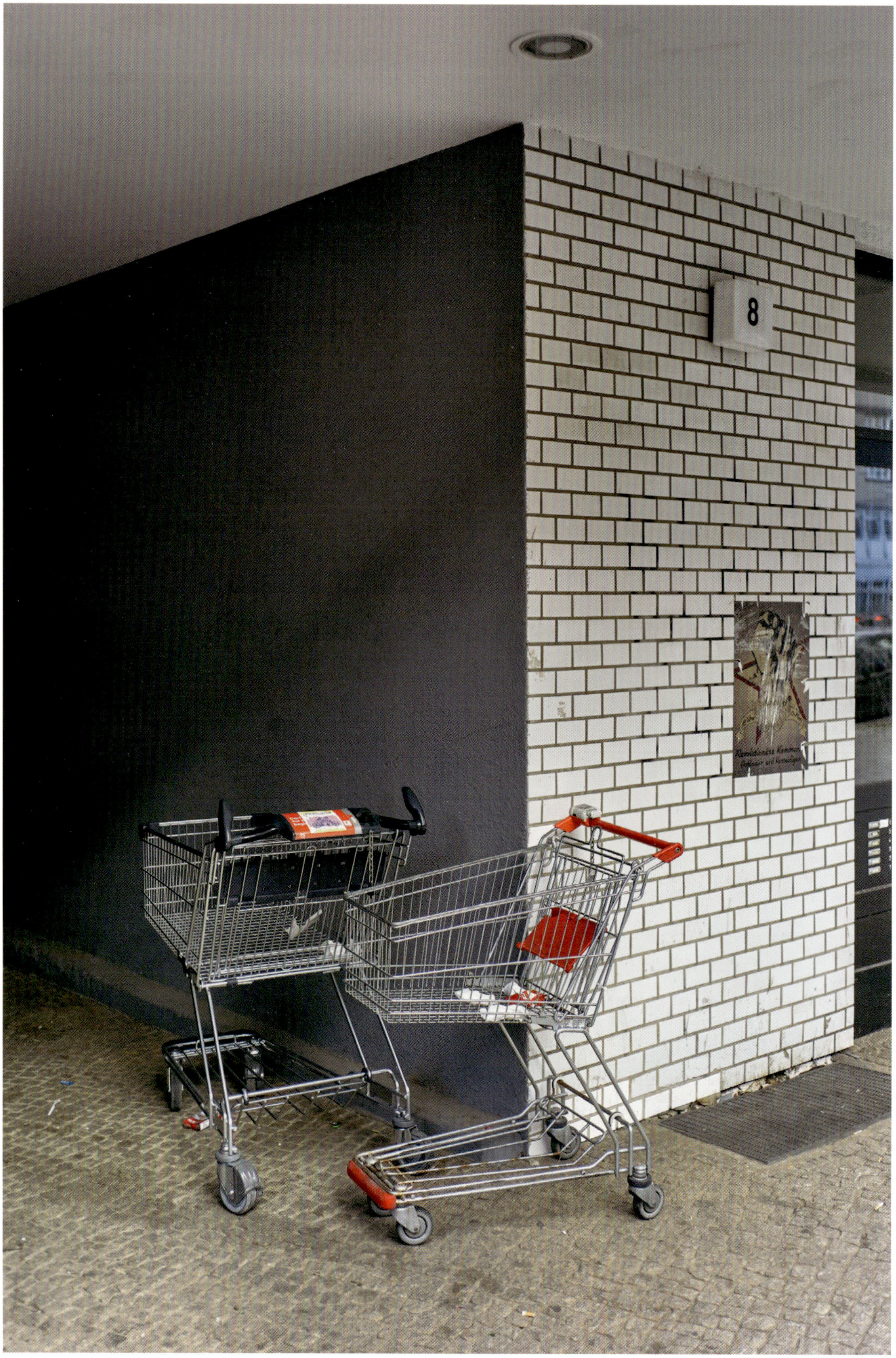
8

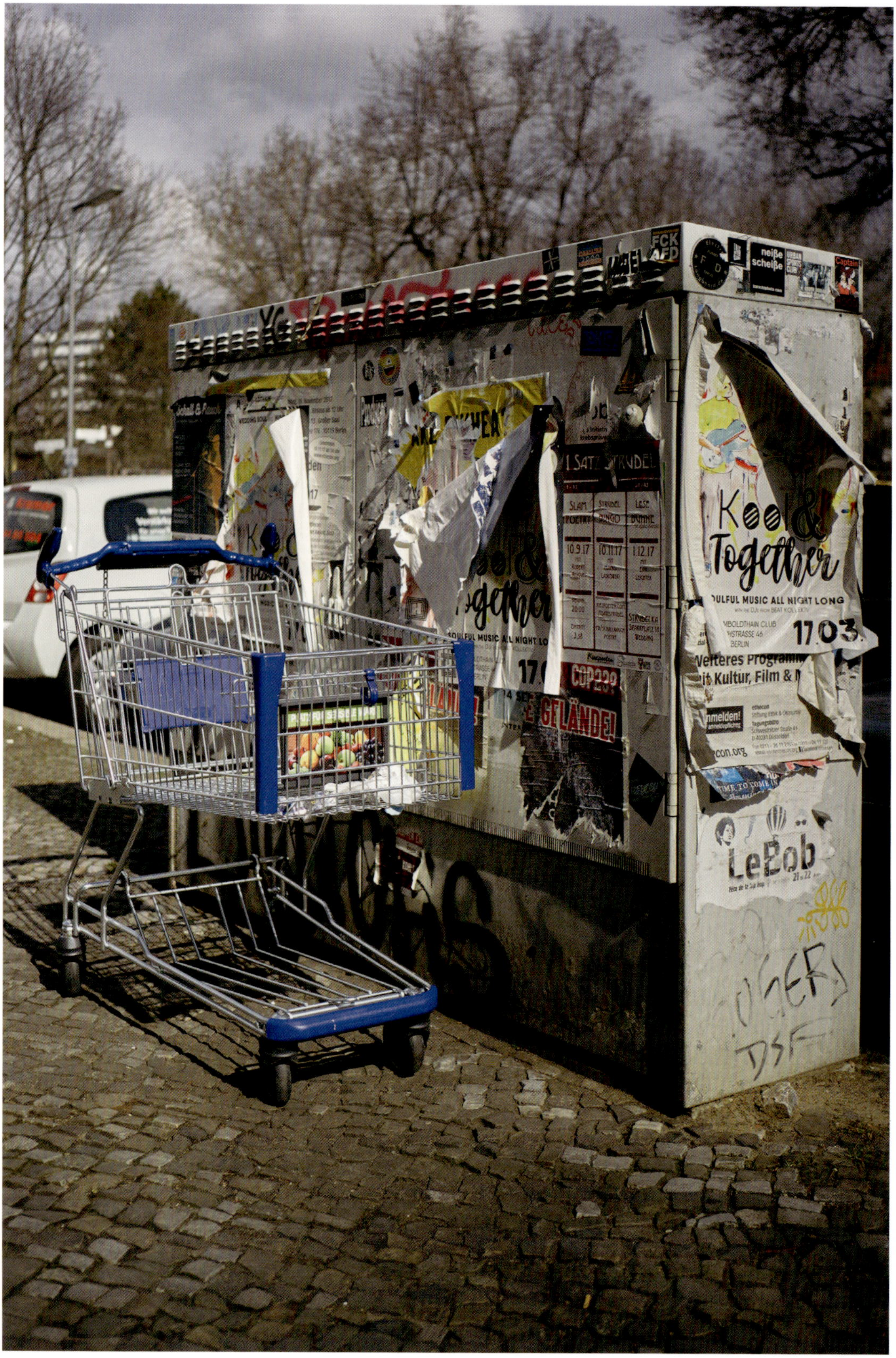
FCK AFD
neiße scheiße
Kool& Together
17.03.
GELÄNDE!
LeBob

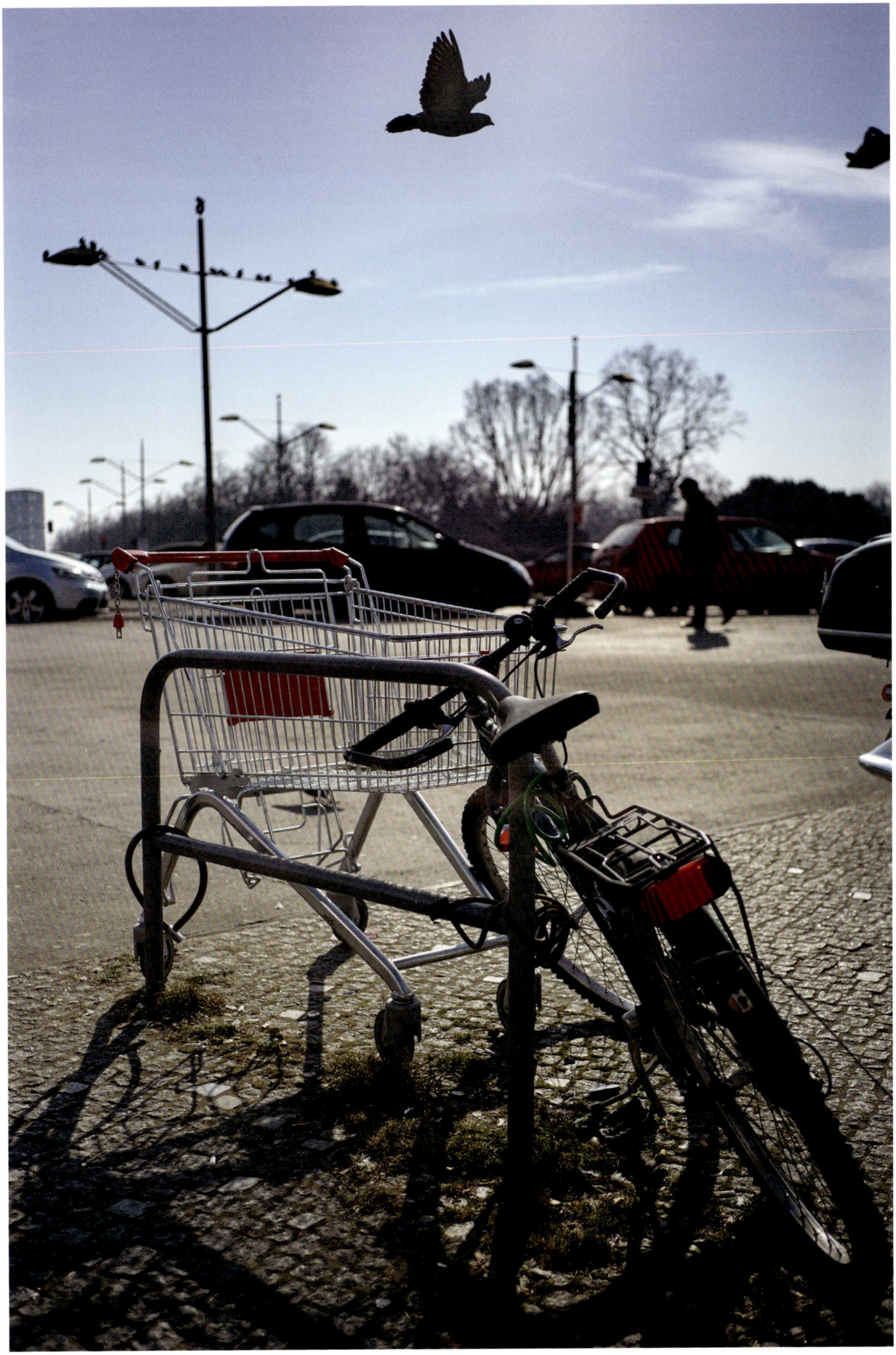

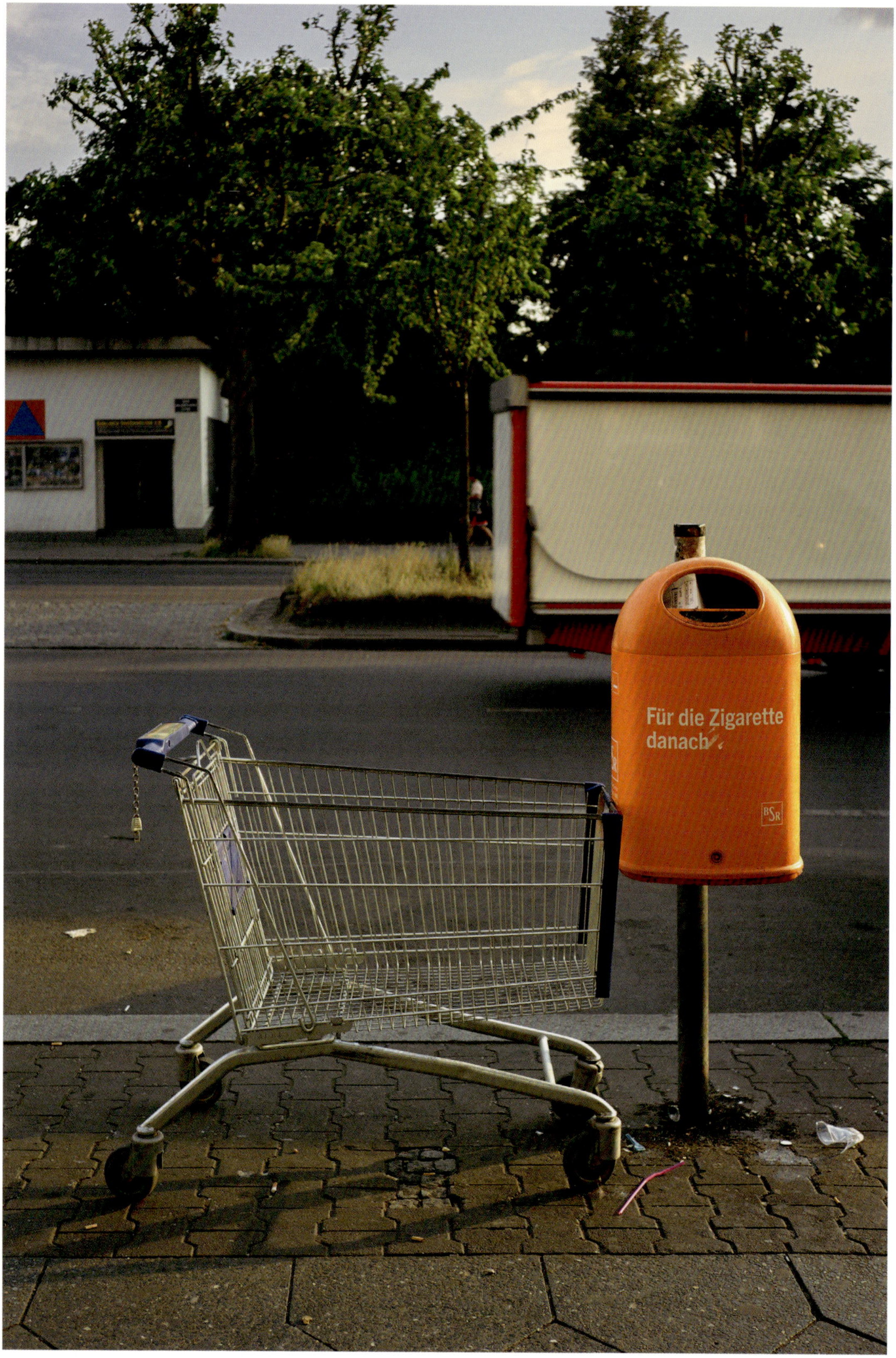
Für die Zigarette
danach

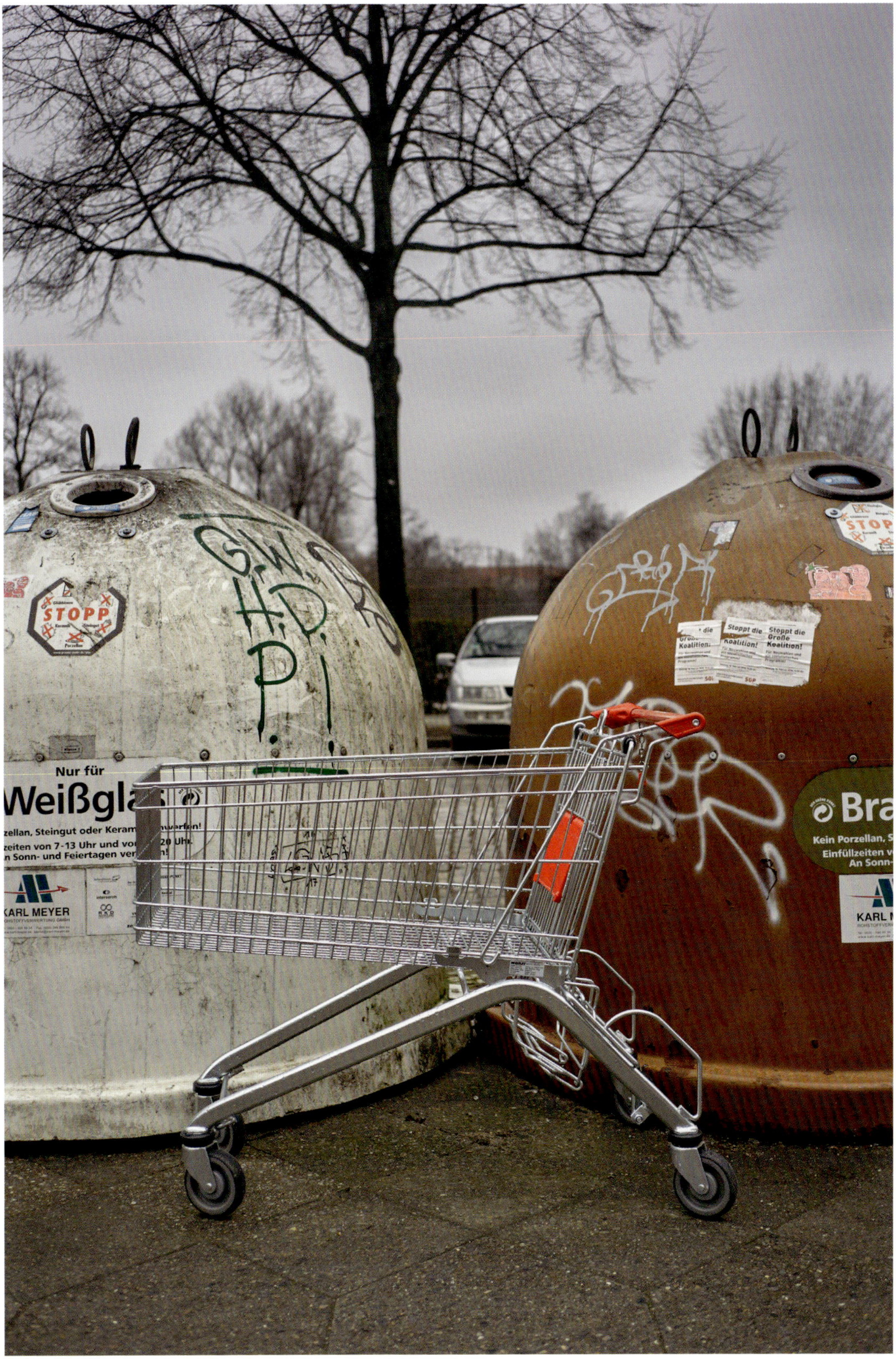
STOPP
Nur für
Weißgla
zellan, Steingut oder Keram
zeiten von 7-13 Uhr und vo
n Sonn- und Feiertagen ve
KARL MEYER
Stoppt die Große Koalition!
Bra
Kein Porzellan, S
Einfüllzeiten v
An Sonn-
KARL M

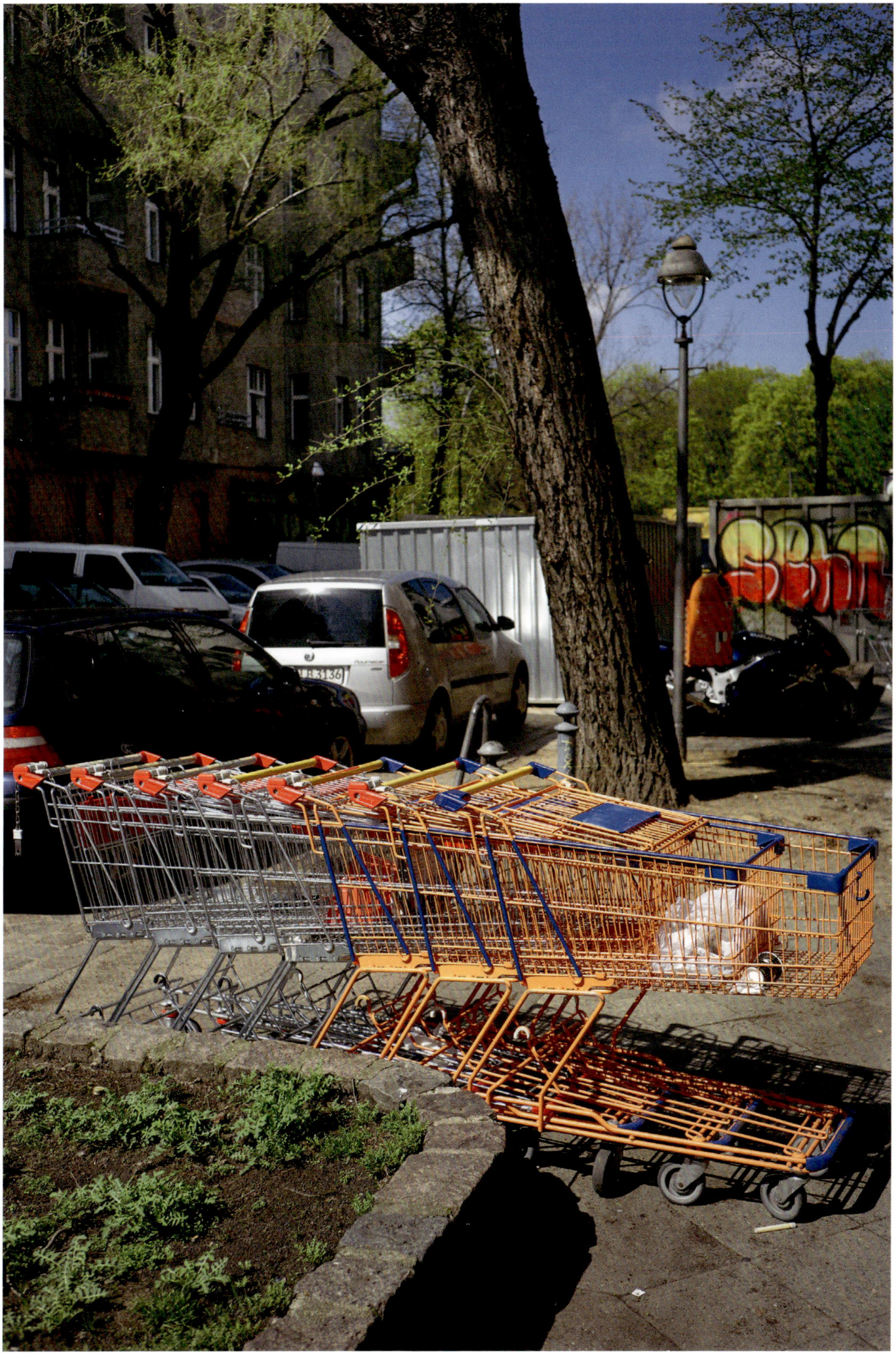

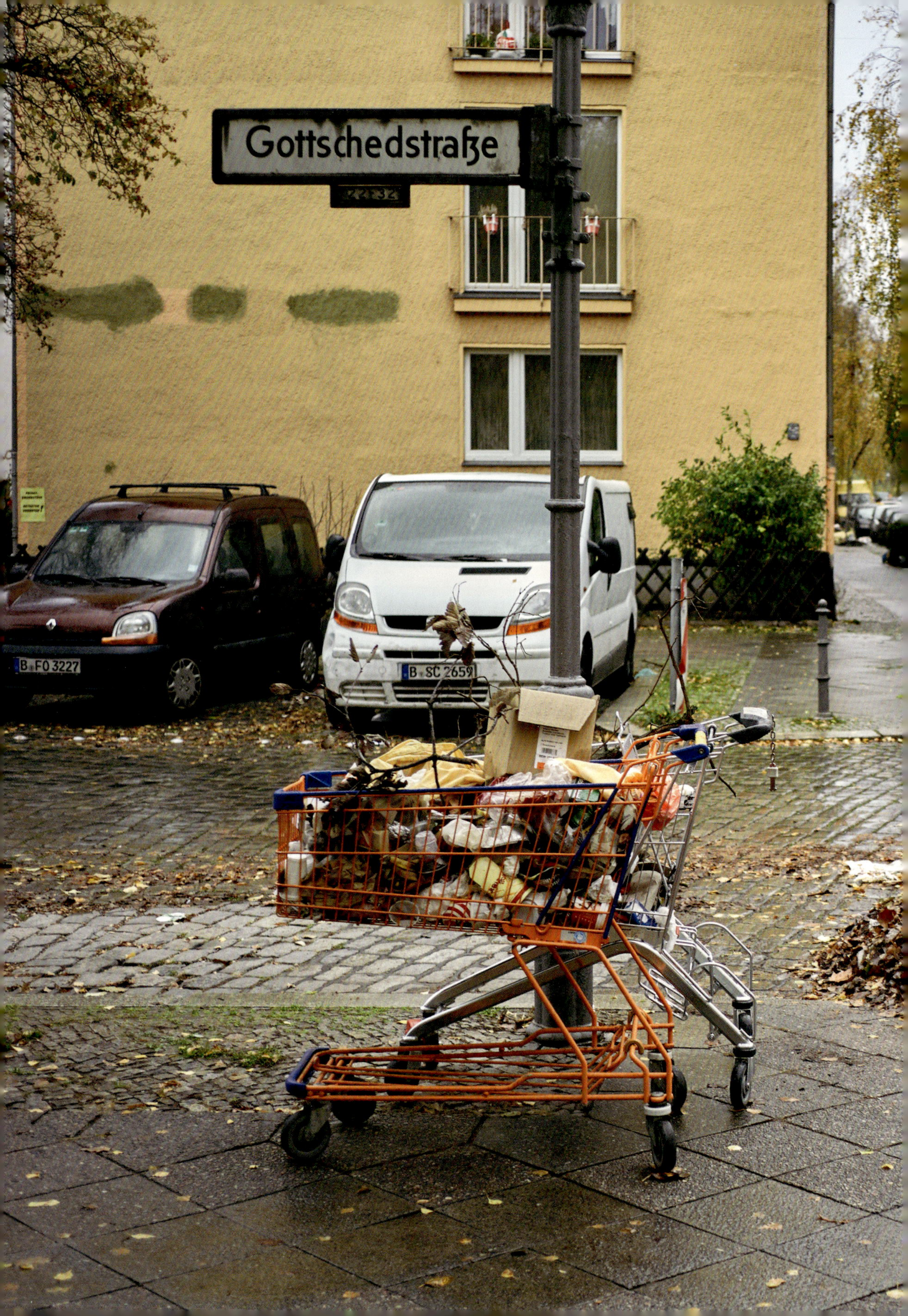
Gottschedstraße
B FO 3227
B SC 2659

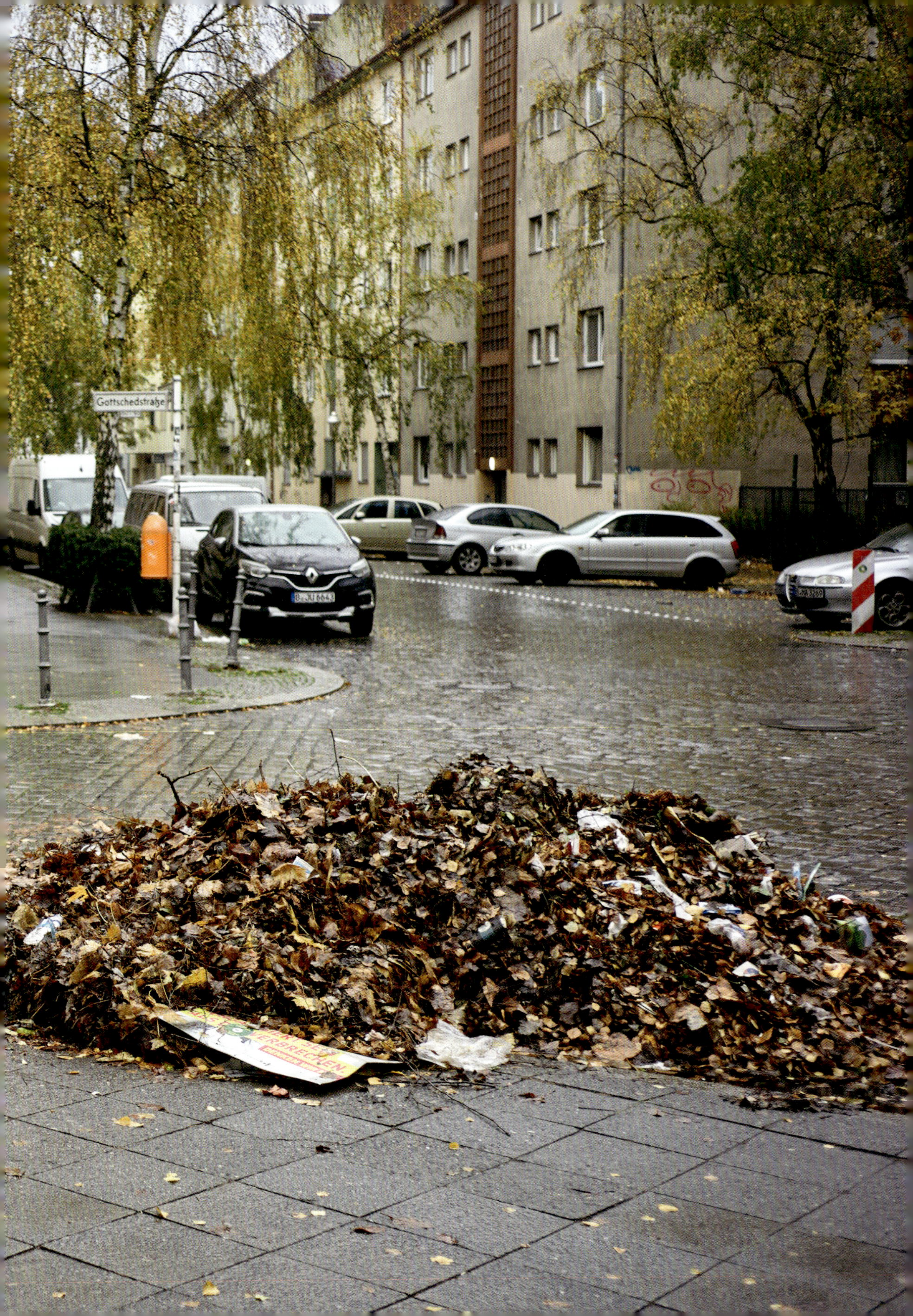
Gottschedstraße

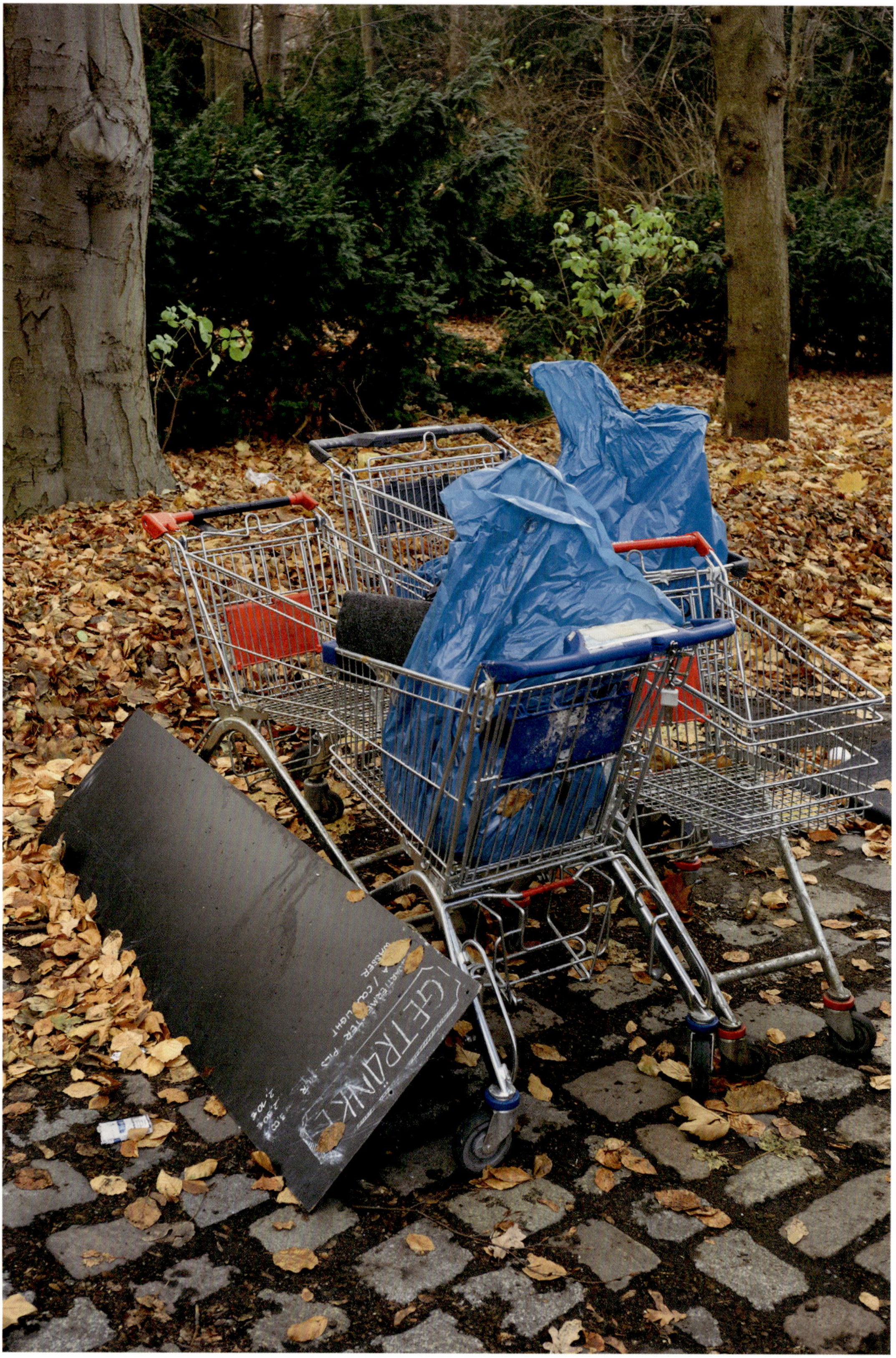
GETRÄNKE

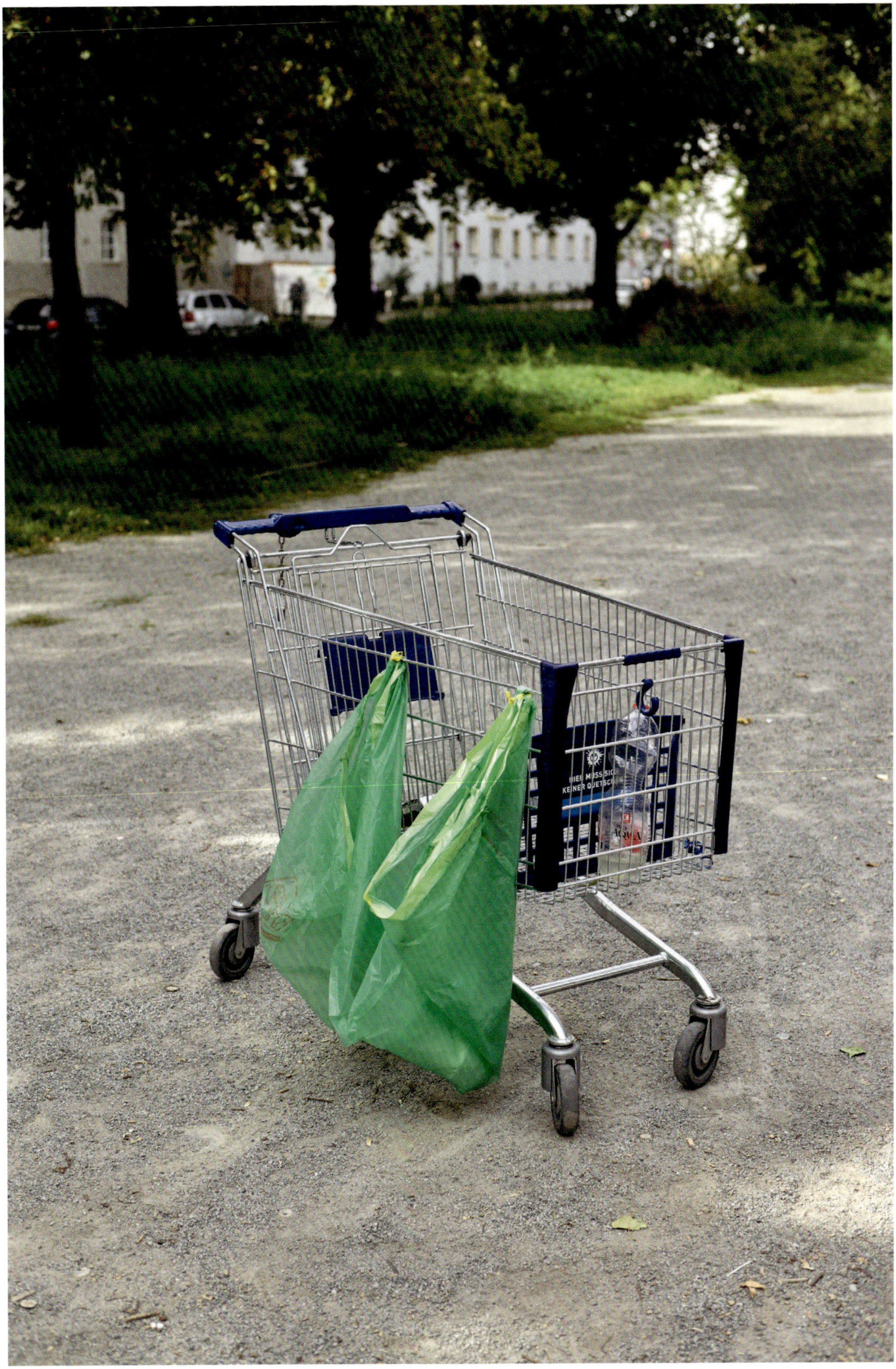

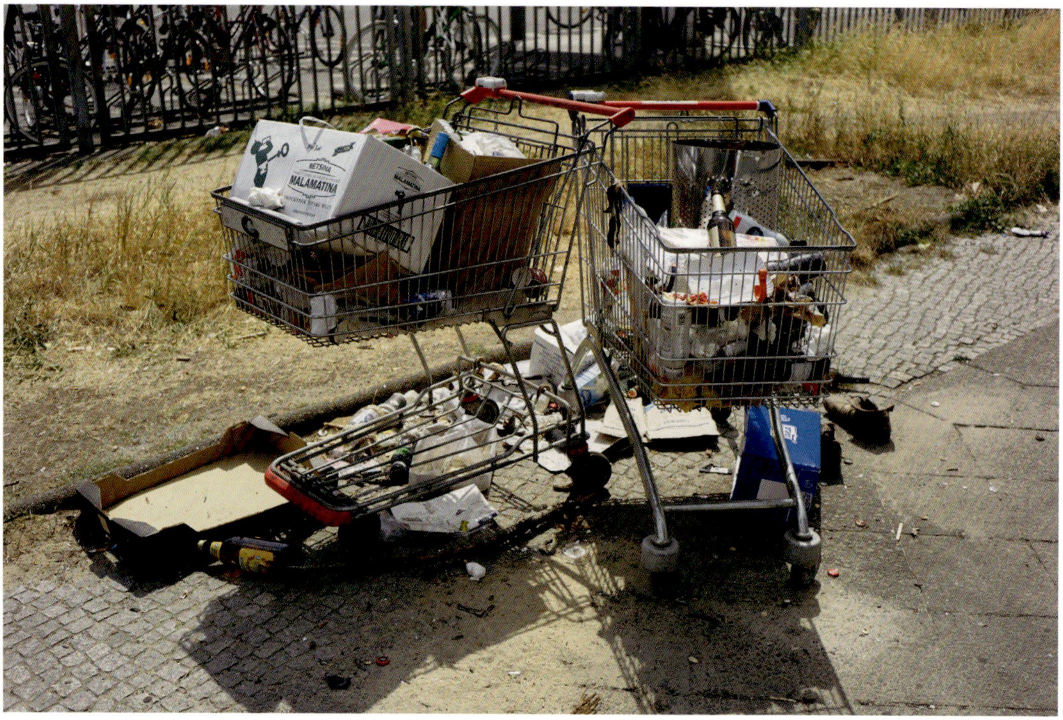
RETSINA
MALAMATINA

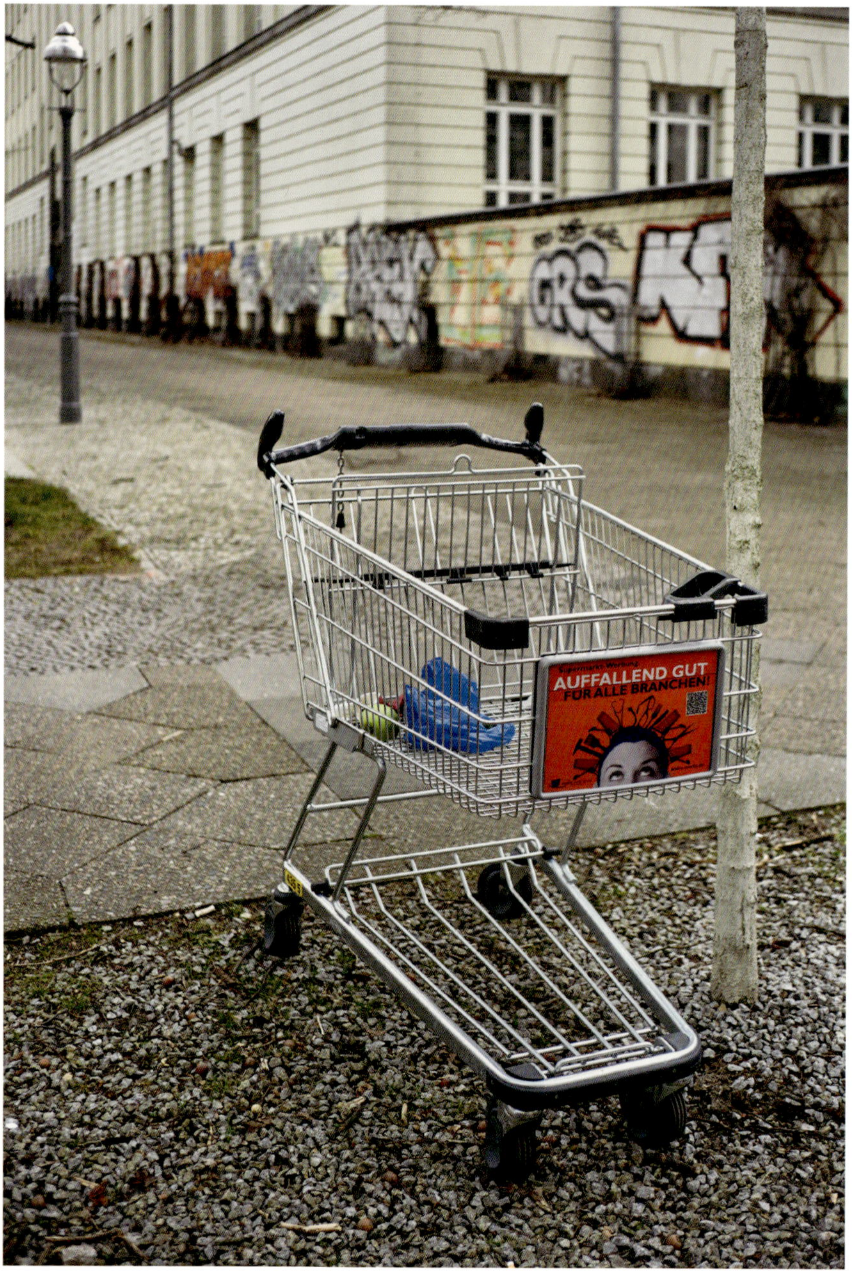
Supermarkt-Werbung
AUFFALLEND GUT
FÜR ALLE BRANCHEN!

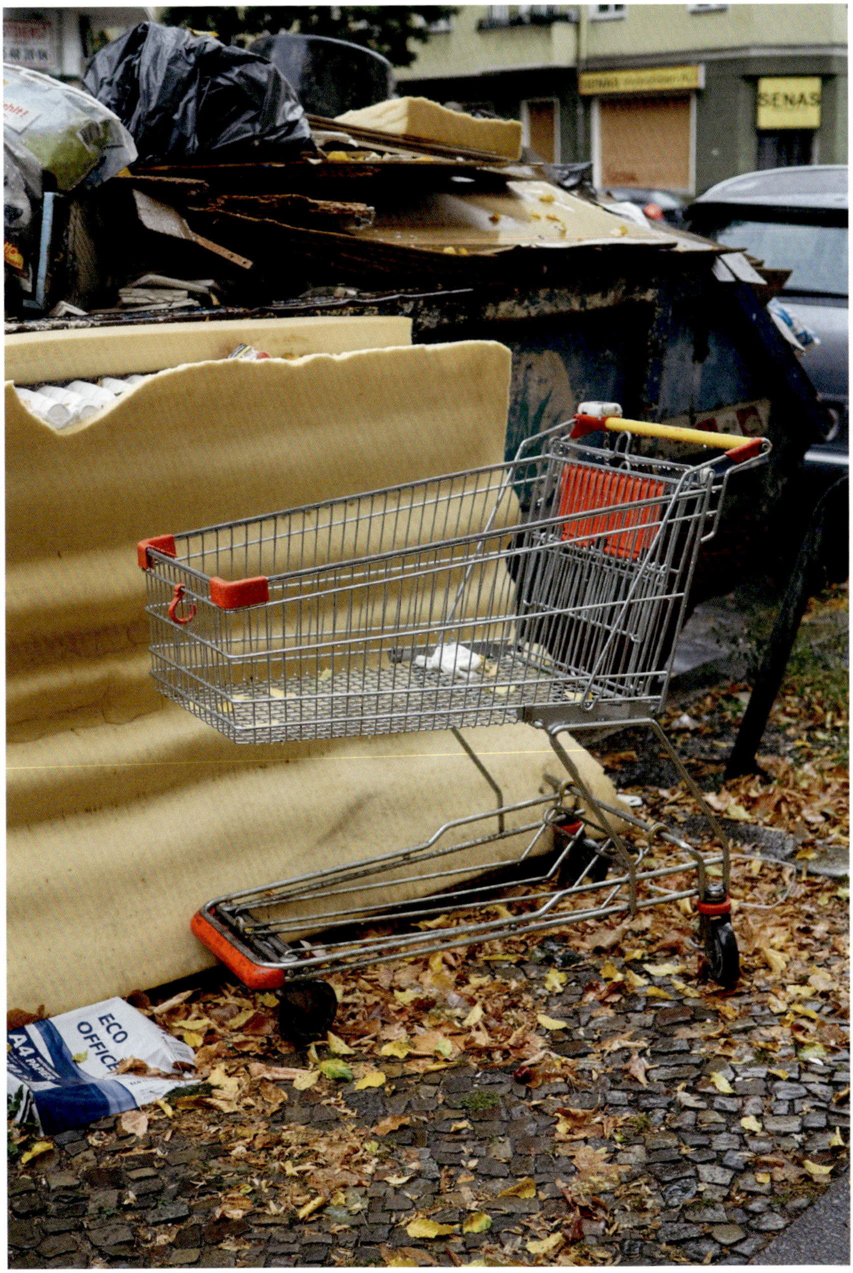
SENAS
ECO
OFFICE
A4

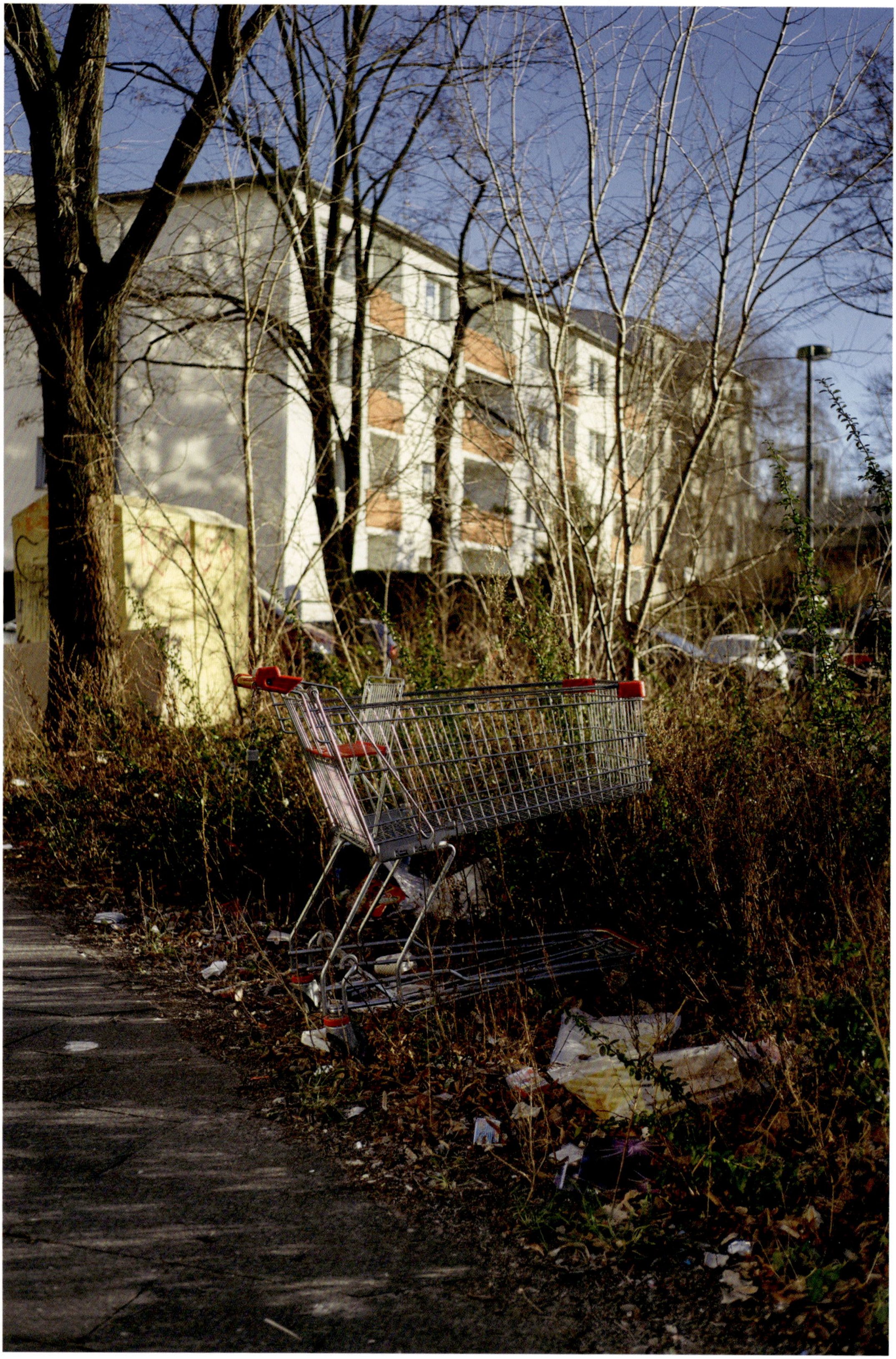

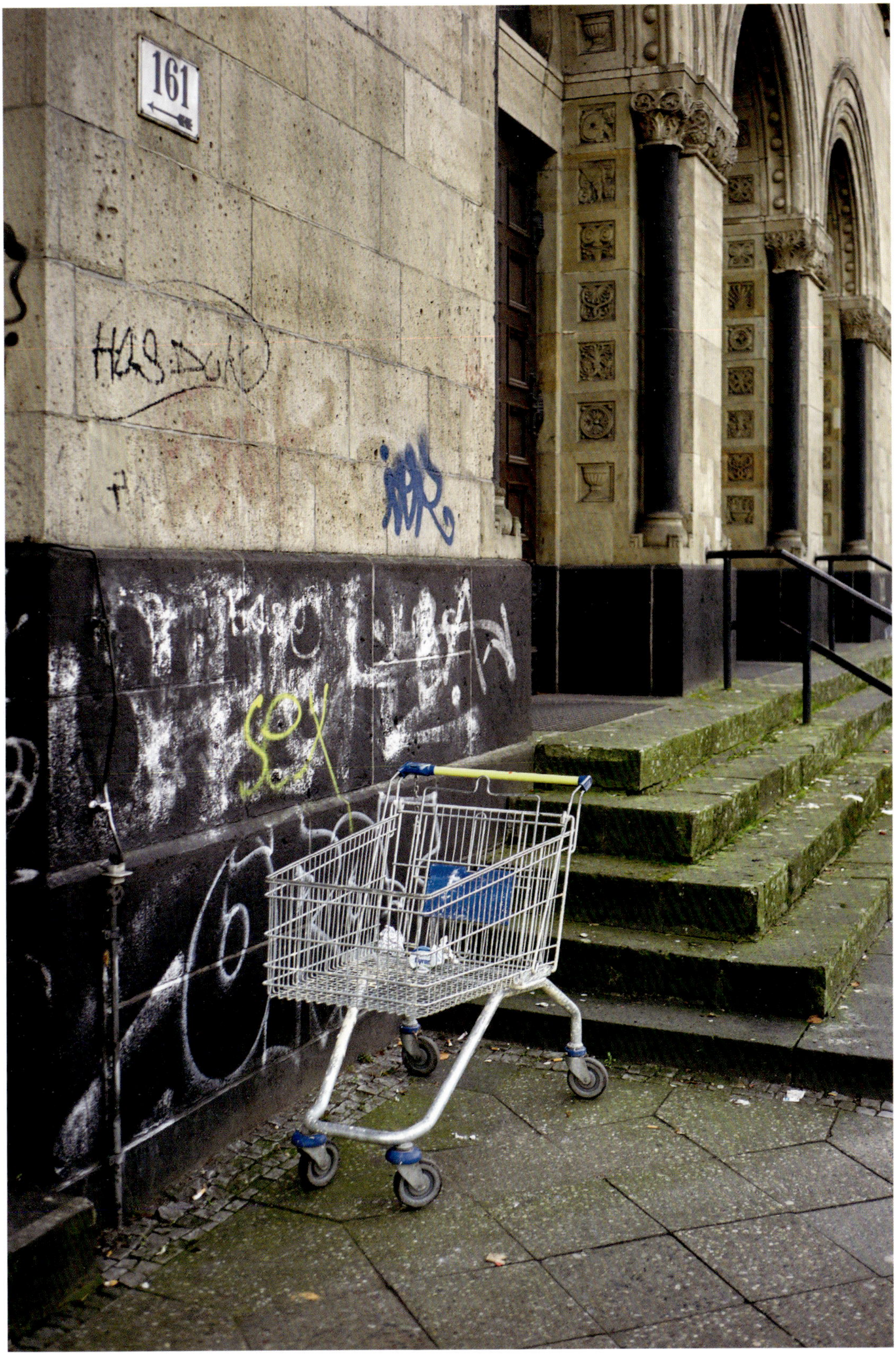
161

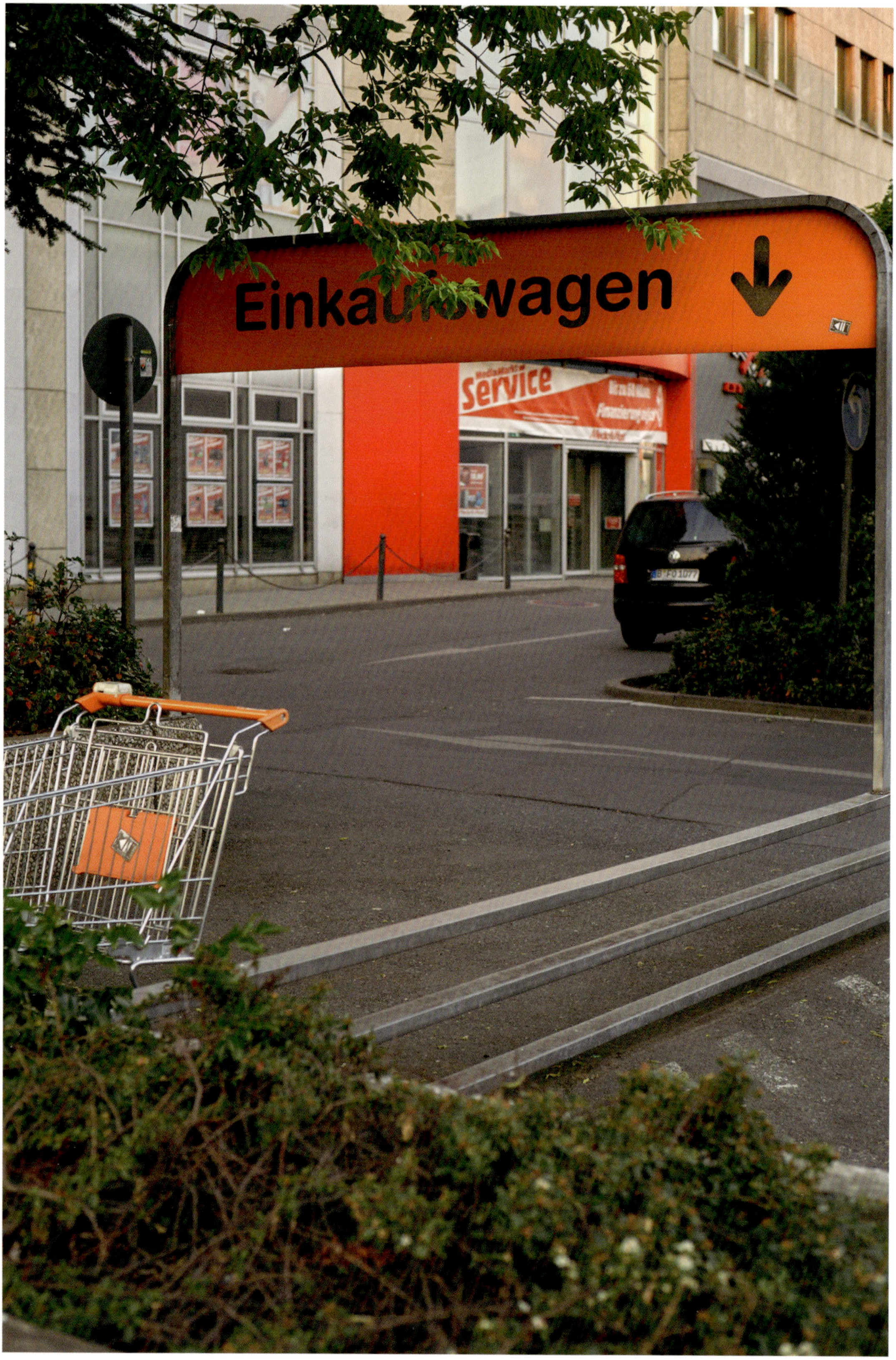
Service

Impressum
Imprint

Fotografien Photographs
Luca Ellena

Einführung Introduction
Tina Wessel

Text
Jonathan Progin

Gestaltung Design
Georg Jaenisch

Lektorat Copy-editing
Tina Wessel, Sarah Quigley

Korrektorat Proofreading
Susann Harring, Sarah Quigley

Übersetzung Translation
Jeanne Haunschild

Projektmanagement Project management Kerber Verlag
Verena Simon

Herstellung Production Kerber Verlag
Jens Bartneck

Gesamtherstellung Printed and published by
Kerber Verlag
Windelsbleicher Str. 166–170
33659 Bielefeld
Germany
Tel. +49 (0) 5 21/9 50 08-10
Fax +49 (0) 5 21/9 50 08-88
info@kerberverlag.com
kerberverlag.com

KERBER Publikationen werden weltweit vertrieben
Kerber publications are distributed worldwide

ACC Art Books
Sandy Lane
Old Martlesham
Woodbridge, IP12 4SD
UK
Tel. +44 1394 38 99 50
Fax +44 1394 38 99 99
accartbooks.com

Artbook | D.A.P.
75 Broad Street, Suite 630
New York, NY 10004
USA
Tel. +1 212 627 19 99
Fax +1 212 627 94 84
artbook.com

AVA Verlagsauslieferung
Scheidegger
Obere Bahnhofstr. 10A
8910 Affoltern am Albis
Switzerland
Tel. +41 44 762 42 41
Fax +41 44 762 42 49
avainfo@ava.ch

KNV Zeitfracht
Verlagsauslieferung
kerber-verlag@knv-zeitfracht.de

Die Deutsche Nationalbibliothek verzeichnet diese Publikation in der Deutschen Nationalbibliografie: dnb.de.
The Deutsche Nationalbibliothek lists this publication in the Deutsche Nationalbibliografie: dnb.de.

ISBN 978-3-7356-0724-9

www.kerberverlag.com

Printed in Germany

Diese Publikation entstand mit freundlicher Unterstützung von This publication was made possible with the kind support of

Kulturkommission Plaffeien

Galerie Monika Wertheimer

KUND

KULTUR NATUR DEUTSCHFREIBURG